CAMBRIDGE LIBRARY COLLECTION

Books of enduring scholarly value

Classics

From the Renaissance to the nineteenth century, Latin and Greek were compulsory subjects in almost all European universities, and most early modern scholars published their research and conducted international correspondence in Latin. Latin had continued in use in Western Europe long after the fall of the Roman empire as the lingua franca of the educated classes and of law, diplomacy, religion and university teaching. The flight of Greek scholars to the West after the fall of Constantinople in 1453 gave impetus to the study of ancient Greek literature and the Greek New Testament. Eventually, just as nineteenth-century reforms of university curricula were beginning to erode this ascendancy, developments in textual criticism and linguistic analysis, and new ways of studying ancient societies, especially archaeology, led to renewed enthusiasm for the Classics. This collection offers works of criticism, interpretation and synthesis by the outstanding scholars of the nineteenth century.

An Essay on the Modern Pronunciation of the Greek and Latin Languages

Sir Uvedale Price (1747–1829) most notably concerned himself with questions of the preservation of natural beauty and harmony in landscape gardening. His *Essay on the Picturesque* (1794) and *Letter to H. Repton* (second edition, 1798) are also reissued in this series. He took on a completely different subject in the present work, published in 1827. Arguing that modern mispronunciation of ancient Greek and Latin damages 'quantity, metre, rhythm, variety, connexion, euphony, articulation and expression', Price proposes a complete reform. Stresses in particular should be applied along the lines followed by the ancients themselves, thereby preserving the appropriate emphases. He recommends that the young be given proper instruction to correct mistakes and to restore texts to their full effect. Praised by Wordsworth as 'most ingenious', this work will be of value to scholars with an interest in classical phonetics.

Cambridge University Press has long been a pioneer in the reissuing of out-of-print titles from its own backlist, producing digital reprints of books that are still sought after by scholars and students but could not be reprinted economically using traditional technology. The Cambridge Library Collection extends this activity to a wider range of books which are still of importance to researchers and professionals, either for the source material they contain, or as landmarks in the history of their academic discipline.

Drawing from the world-renowned collections in the Cambridge University Library and other partner libraries, and guided by the advice of experts in each subject area, Cambridge University Press is using state-of-the-art scanning machines in its own Printing House to capture the content of each book selected for inclusion. The files are processed to give a consistently clear, crisp image, and the books finished to the high quality standard for which the Press is recognised around the world. The latest print-on-demand technology ensures that the books will remain available indefinitely, and that orders for single or multiple copies can quickly be supplied.

The Cambridge Library Collection brings back to life books of enduring scholarly value (including out-of-copyright works originally issued by other publishers) across a wide range of disciplines in the humanities and social sciences and in science and technology.

An Essay on the Modern Pronunciation of the Greek and Latin Languages

UVEDALE PRICE

CAMBRIDGE UNIVERSITY PRESS

CAMBRIDGE
UNIVERSITY PRESS

University Printing House, Cambridge, CB2 8BS, United Kingdom

Published in the United States of America by Cambridge University Press, New York

Cambridge University Press is part of the University of Cambridge.
It furthers the University's mission by disseminating knowledge in the pursuit of
education, learning and research at the highest international levels of excellence.

www.cambridge.org
Information on this title: www.cambridge.org/9781108067140

© in this compilation Cambridge University Press 2014

This edition first published 1827
This digitally printed version 2014

ISBN 978-1-108-06714-0 Paperback

AN

ESSAY,

&c.

AN

ESSAY

ON THE

MODERN PRONUNCIATION

OF THE

GREEK AND LATIN LANGUAGES.

BY

UVEDALE PRICE, Esq.

Οἱ παλαιοὶ ἄλλως ἐξεφώνουν τὸ μακρὸν, καὶ ἄλλως τὸ βραχυ.

Vet. Grammat.

OXFORD,
PRINTED BY W. BAXTER.
1827.

PREFACE.

THIS small volume is a part only, but a
considerable part, of what I have written
on the subject; it contains, however, the
leading positions and principles upon which
my notions are founded. I thought it best
to print, but not to publish, it, in the hope
that some of the learned persons who will
receive it, may think it has sufficient merit
and interest to deserve their notice, and
may be induced to put down their remarks and criticisms as they occur, and to
favour me with a sight of them; in such
a case, I should afterwards, with much
more confidence, submit the whole to the
public eye. The errors committed by the
moderns in pronouncing the ancient lan-

guages, have at various periods been occasionally pointed out by men of great learning and high reputation: by Erasmus, Metcherchus, and in our own times by Foster, in his excellent work on accent and quantity, and by Bishop Horsley; and the whole of a small book, entitled Metronariston, and supposed to be written by Dr. Warner, is on the subject of our errors. In this last, there are many just remarks, and many apt examples and illustrations, which I have freely made use of; but there is no plan, and the style is diffuse and full of singularities. As to myself, I must frankly own, that I have not the most distant pretension to erudition, or to that extent of reading that seems requisite for an undertaking of this kind; my hope is, that great zeal, and an unremitting attention to the subject for several years, may in some measure compensate my deficiencies. As this confession, however, is not calculated to give a favourable impression of my performance, and as I should be sorry to mar it at the very outset, I will mention that some persons of undoubted and extensive erudition, particularly my much regretted friends, Mr. Knight and Dr. Parr, had looked over a considerable part of what I had written, and gave me their valuable advice and assistance, as well as their encouragement. Mine is direct, undisguised, and unqualified attack on the whole and every part of our system. In the arrangement of my materials, I have endeavoured to pursue such a plan, as may enable the reader to follow the several points without difficulty or distraction. The charges I have to bring are numerous and weighty: I hope to shew clearly, that by our mode of pronouncing the Greek and Latin, we injure, to a very great and extensive degree, quantity, metre, rhythm, variety, connexion, euphony, articulation, and expression. If I fail in my proofs, I neither deserve nor expect any mercy; but if I succeed, what shall we say to such a catalogue of enormities? I would say, in the words of Hamlet, " O, reform it al- together."

My chief object is, of course, our own pronunciation: but I shall at the same time consider, though with much more diffidence, and under correction, that of the Italians. No one can hear an Italian recite Latin verses, without being struck and pleased with the open sound of the vowels, the full tone and length given to the long syllables, the force and lightness of their trochees and dactyls, and the general harmony and charm of their utterance. These are high excellences, and of the most seducing kind: I was led, however, to observe, especially since I turned my thoughts to the subject, that they laid their accent on the same syllables upon which we lay our's; and in the course of the following pages I shall produce some convincing proofs, that, as far as the position of the accents is concerned, their pronunciation is the very same as our's. I have indeed strong reasons for thinking, that at a particular period we were induced to adopt their mode altogether, abandoning one of a totally different character, which we had uniformly practised from the time of the Conquest to that of Chaucer, and long afterwards. This is a curious matter of enquiry, but which I shall reserve for a future occasion. I am well aware that my open attack on what is called pronouncing by *accent* in contradistinction to *quantity*, will offend numbers of my own countrymen, and almost all the Italians; as, from various circumstances, they are very naturally led to suppose that their pronunciation of the Latin is perfect in all, as it is in most, respects; but as there are among them many candid and liberal, as well as learned and ingenious persons, from such I may hope for a fair and dispassionate examination of my positions and arguments, notwithstanding early habits and prepossessions. One Italian,

whose reputation for critical knowledge
both of ancient and modern literature is of
the highest kind, Signor Ugo Foscolo, after
having read the principal part of what I
have written, freely declared that his principles agreed with mine; and he is "himself a host."

With respect to the Greek, I am very
much at a loss: I have never had an opportunity of hearing it pronounced by an
Italian, nor have I met with any precise
account of their mode of accenting it. I
am indeed led to suppose, that we received
from them, and at the same period, our
mode of accenting both languages: this is
mere conjecture; but till I can gain more
accurate information on the subject, I must
be allowed to presume, for the sake of
continuing the general argument without
frequent restrictions and explanations, that
the Italian mode of accenting both the
ancient languages is the same as our's;
wishing it to be understood, that when I

say *we* lay the accent, I only mean to speak positively of the English; of the Italians only conditionally, and subject to correction. It is presumed in this Preface, first, that the English lay an accent on the same syllables on which the Italians lay it; secondly, that the accent has the same effect in both languages, that of lengthening the syllable upon which it is laid; thirdly, that by the mode in which it is laid, the pronunciation of the Greek and Latin is greatly injured in various points, especially in the very material one of quantity. Accent and quantity, as we all know, were the great regulators of ancient pronunciation[a]: with quantity, and the rules which relate to it, we are thoroughly acquainted, and never pass over the slightest

---

[a] I have, for obvious reasons, avoided all marking of the Greek accents: they have no effect on our pronunciation, and would only serve to complicate the already complicated marks: that of the lene breathing, as being unnecessary, I have omitted for the same reasons.

offence against them in the structure of verses, whatever we may do in their recitation. My first enquiry then (a very short one) will be, what constitutes ancient accent: my second, a much longer, what constitutes modern accent, and in what the difference between the two prinpally consists.

CONTENTS.

———

AN

ESSAY

ON THE

MODERN PRONUNCIATION

OF THE

GREEK AND LATIN LANGUAGES.

ANCIENT ACCENT.

ANCIENT accent, according to the best critics, consisted in the elevation, depression, and inflection of the
voice on the accented syllables, and did not interfere
with the settled quantity or length of those syllables:
this very material point is set forth and explained in
the clearest and most satisfactory manner by Foster, in
his excellent work on Accent and Quantity. Thus, for
instance, the acute accent was on the first and short
syllables of the iambi ἄνᾰξ and sĕ'nēx, on the first and
second of the anapæsts μĕγᾰ'λῶν and rĕ'cŭbāns, and the
voice, as it easily might, was raised upon them; but
they remained equally short, and in both cases the voice
passed rapidly to the long final syllable, on which, but
in a lower or graver tone, it fully rested.

On the subject of modern accent the opinions of
several eminent critics are widely at variance. Lord
Montboddo, in his very curious and learned work
on the Origin of Languages, gives his opinion decidedly, that accented syllables in English, are, in our
pronunciation, *not* made *longer*, but only *louder*,
than the unaccented; and Mr. Mitford, in his ingenious and instructive Essay on the Harmony of Languages, maintains, that our accent does *not* give length.
On the other hand, Johnson considers the acute tone

B

and long quantity in English metre as the same: and Foster, who quotes this opinion, says himself, " notwithstanding the confidence with which it is often affirmed that the English metre depends on accent, and not on quantity, which I have endeavoured to refute, and though I have seemed to allow that accent jointly with quantity doth direct it, yet I cannot help thinking that the essence of it is founded on quantity alone[a]." My own opinion, which, at least, has not been hastily or inconsiderately taken up, or in mere deference to any authority, completely coincides with that of Johnson and of Foster: but, as men of the greatest learning and ingenuity so widely differ from one another, and as the point itself is of the utmost consequence in respect to the subject on which I have undertaken to write, I may be allowed to offer what has occurred to me on this disputed point.

All words in our language of more than one syllable have an accent on one of them, and in most cases on one only; that is, according to the doctrine just laid down, one syllable in each word is long; the others (with some exceptions which shall be noticed) comparatively short: our dissyllables therefore are almost all of them either trochees or iambi; these last, such as *alóne, beréft, careér*, &c. are, in my mind, truly

---

[a] This is confirmed (says Foster, page 37.) by the decisive authority of Mr. Johnson, whose very great abilities and extensive erudition have done honour to his age and country. He, in the rules of his prosody prefixed to his Dictionary, considers the acute tone and long quantity on English metre and rhythm as the *same*.

iambi, according to ancient prosody, the last syllable
being about twice the length of the first. Our anapæsts
likewise, as *serenáde, legatée,* are truly such, the last
syllable being nearly equal to the two first; and both
these feet in English, as we pronounce them, might
serve as standards for the pronunciation of iambi and
anapæsts in Greek and Latin. Should this be questioned, I would ask, how the quantity of either of these
feet could be more truly expressed? or in what manner
our pronunciation of such words as have been instanced
could be altered, so as to be better suited to that
quantity? I think it can scarcely be questioned; and
if admitted, then accented syllables in such English
words are decidedly longer than the *un*accented, and
there is an end of the dispute. It is true that we
generally sound the accented syllable more strongly
than the unaccented; and the natural inference is,
that such syllables are longer: in the first place, it is
much more easy to lay a stress, and to lay it with
effect, on a long syllable upon which the voice can
dwell, than on a short one, over which it must pass
rapidly; and, indeed, it requires some effort, and also
some address, to give strength and loudness to a mere
passing note, and still to preserve its shortness. In
the second place, the long syllable (for in English we
have seldom more than one in the same word) is *that*
which gives it its character; and therefore we are always
inclined to lay an emphasis upon it; and we have the
double motive of being able to do it with most ease, and
most effect. Lord Montboddo's first general position,

as I have already stated, is, that our accent gives loudness, not length; his second, (which flows from the first,) that our English metre depends solely on the *stress* laid on the accented syllables, not on their *duration*; and a third, in support of the two others, is, that you may alter the length of syllables in English verse without injuring the metre: and if this last position were universally true, instead of being partially so, and chiefly in regard to monosyllables, it would very strongly support the others. From the laxity of our prosody, compared with the strictness of that of the ancients, a shorter syllable may often be substituted in our verses for a longer, especially in lines where there are many monosyllables; as in such words, none of them having an accent, no comparison can be made between accented and unaccented syllables. The line which Lord Montboddo has given as an example, (the first of the Paradise Lost,) out of seven words, has six monosyllables; but the question is about accented syllables, and I shall take my example from the fifth line of the same poem:

Restóre us, and regaín that blíssful seat.

If it be true that loudness, or stress, is the essence of our accent, then, if both the syllables of any of these words be pronounced with an equal tone, there can be no accent on either, although you should make a decided difference in their length; the experiment is easily tried; and I think I may answer for it, that if you make the last syllable in *regaín* decidedly long, sounding it as softly as possible, and the first as decidedly short, giving it as much strength as you can contrive to give to a short syllable, the *accent*, as every one will acknowledge, will be in its usual place. Again, let the experiment be reversed : give length to *re*, and strength to *gain*, and *re* will clearly be the accented syllable ; and rĕgaĭ'n, from a manifest iambus, will be changed into rē'gaĭn as manifest a trochee ; and every one will perceive that the accent (in fact the quantity) is false. In the same manner you may turn *blissful* from a trochee into an iambus, by passing quickly over the first syllable, and dwelling upon the last. The experiment is still better made in words of more than two syllables, as in the concluding anapæst of the following line :

And the whispering sound of the cool colonade.

Pronounce *co* long, as in *cólon*, (for if you pass on to the consonant, it is difficult to prolong the sound,) and as softly as you can, and the two last syllables shortly and loudly, the anapæst will be reversed, and turned into a dactyl, cō'lŏnăde, and the metre and rhythm turned topsy-turvy. Try the same experiment on the middle syllable, and you will have an amphibrachys, cŏlō'năde.

If the truth of these statements be admitted, or cannot be disproved, the essence of English accent, as Foster maintains, is *quantity;* and *loudness*, a natural, but not a necessary, consequence of length[b]; and the

---

[b] We generally, for the reasons that have been mentioned, lay a stress on the accented syllables; but there are passages where a nearly equal tone

acute tone and long quantity in English metre, as Johnson asserts, is the same.

The great source of error and misconception throughout is the term *accent;* as it gives a wrong bias, and leads us to think of any thing rather than quantity; and it particularly leads us towards its ancient signification—the higher and lower tones of voice used in speaking. It may therefore be said, by those who have this last-mentioned bias, " Admitting that we do make the accented syllable longer than the unaccented, yet the right *accent* in such words must be distinguished, not by the different *length* of the two syllables, but by the different *pitch of the voice* on the last." This is what I shall now examine: my creed, the same as Foster's, is, that quantity is the essence of what is called accent; and my position, that while the *length* of the accented syllables is preserved the accent is right; and wrong whenever the length is changed. Let us suppose, then, a person, who expected to hear the worst news of an absent and dying friend, eagerly to ask the messenger, " Was he alive?" In such a case he would naturally raise his voice on the last syllable to its highest pitch.

throughout, though it would diminish the effect of particular words, might perhaps give a more characteristic expression to the whole. This is particularly the case where there is any thing of mystery, as in a line of Shakespear's Hamlet:

> This to me
> In dreadful secrecy impart they did.

And no one, for want of emphasis, could doubt whether the accents were right or wrong.

If we again suppose the answer to be given in a low despondent tone, that scarcely left any hope, " He was alive," the voice would as naturally be depressed to its lowest pitch. Here then are the two extremes of acute and grave on the same syllable; yet while its *length* was preserved, every one would feel that the *accent* was right, and equally so both in the question and the answer. But let this accent, as it is called, be laid on the first syllable; " Was he ā'lĭve?" " He was ā'lĭve;" whatever might be the pitch of the voice, however it might be modified, whether in question and answer, or any other form of speech, every one would instantly feel that the *accent* or quantity was false. I will now, begging for indulgence, risk an Italian example of a similar kind: and shall suppose an Italian, who had just witnessed a violent quarrel between two persons, and was giving an account of it to one who felt an interest in both the parties, to say to him, " e tirando un suo pugnale, lo ferì nel petto:" I imagine that he would in such a sentence pronounce the last syllable of *ferì* nearly in the same even tone as the first. If we then suppose the hearer to exclaim, " Come! lo ferì!" the voice would almost necessarily be raised to its highest pitch; and that of the first speaker equally depressed, if he answered in an assenting but melancholy tone, " *Si, lo ferì*." Here then, if I am right in what I have advanced, we have the extreme of the acute and of the grave, and also a middle tone between both; yet I think I may venture to say, that the *accent* would be right, as long as the *quantity* of the last syllable was preserved: but lay the accent on the first syllable, *féri*, by which it evidently becomes long, and the last short, and instantly, with the change of quantity, the accent becomes false, the sense of the word is changed, and that of the sentence destroyed, in whatever way the voice may be elevated, depressed, or modulated. The English and Italian examples just given were of course made for the occasion: but any person who will repeat a few English verses, carefully observing, what is seldom or never observed, the pitch of his voice on the different syllables, will find that when he does raise it on an acuted syllable, he generally continues it on the next, sometimes on the two next, upon the same level; and that on many accented syllables he evidently drops, instead of raising, his voice. I will mention one out of a thousand examples.

Who first seduc'd them to that foul revolt?

The voice is raised on *first*, a monosyllable, and therefore not acuted; it is lowered on *se*, and raised on the acuted *dúc'd*, but continued on the unaccented *them;* it is lowered on *to that*, raised on *foul*, continued on the *un*accented *re*, and at once decidedly lowered on the acuted *vólt*. Our accent, therefore, does not indicate elevation, or depression, for it cannot indicate both. I believe it to be very much the same in Italian: the accent they made use of in writing and in print is in form the grave; if I am not mistaken, however, the voice is as often elevated as depressed upon it; but the syllable is always long.

These instances (and many more of various kinds might easily be given) furnish, in my mind, a clear and undeniable proof, that quantity is the essence of modern accent; the voice being variously raised or depressed on the accented syllable, as the occasion might require; the length of the syllable on no occasion ever changed.

The fact is, and it gives additional weight to what has been advanced, that in English we have no other way of indicating long and short syllables, but by placing the acute mark over the long, and leaving the short without any mark; and this, as we have seldom more than one accented or long syllable in the same word, is generally sufficient. We have, however, not a few polysyllables, in which there are two of nearly equal length, though what may be called the *primary* accent alone is marked; they are for the most part compound words, in which the addition alters or modifies the sense of the simple; as *unresérv'd*, or, as in a line of Milton's,

> When insuppórtably his foot advanc'd.

In such cases we give a nearly equal length to both the syllables in question, and a greater emphasis, as the expression obviously inquires, to the additional one.

In Italian, according to the grammars of that language, there are two accentual marks, the acute and the grave, though the grave only is in common use: it is never placed but on final syllables, which are always long. In dissyllables, when this mark is not on the last, the first syllable, though not marked, is of course

accented and long, and in grammars is sometimes distinguished by an acute; though both marks, I believe,
equally indicate length, and little, if any thing, else.
The difference of length in the two syllables is the sole
distinction in dissyllabic verbs, between words consist-
ing of the very same letters, but differing in tense, and
person, and sometimes in mood: as ámo, amò, péri,
perì; those accented on the first being perfect trochees,
those on the last perfect iambi, and both of them
standards for the pronunciation of the same feet in the
ancient languages. The Italians have many polysyllables, which like ours have two distinctly accented
syllables, though sometimes neither of them is marked,
sometimes one; as, rimproverare, rimproveràr; in all
such words, whether English or Italian, an accentual
mark (no matter what the form, whether of the acute
or the grave) placed on the long syllables *only*, would
indicate the quantity throughout the whole, the unaccented syllables being short, as in únresérv'd, ínsup-
pórtably, réstoràr, íntenirìr, rímproveráre. These accentual marks would equally serve to indicate the quantity in Greek and Latin words: ἀργαλεών, ἀργαλεοίο,
ímperitáns, ímperitáre, ínsoléntia: and on the other
hand, the ancient marks would just as well indicate the
pronunciation of the English and Italian words; as,
ūnrĕsērv'd, īnsŭppōrtăblў, rīmprŏvĕrār, īntĕnĭrīr; and no
one accustomed to such marks would hesitate as to the
pronunciation. All this, after having considered every
part with the best attention I could give it, appears to
me clear and satisfactory: should it appear so to others,

then modern accent and ancient quantity, the marks being convertible, are completely identified; for I do not see how any stronger proof of identity can be given, than such convertibility. On these grounds, which will occasionally be farther illustrated and confirmed, I shall assume, that our accent, under a misleading name, is simply quantity; that our versification is regulated by it as *such*, and not, as has so strenuously been maintained, by accent, as something distinct from quantity, and even opposed to it; and that ancient versification, avowedly regulated by means of long and short syllables, is neither more nor less so than ours, though in a stricter manner and degree. No one certainly ever pretended that all the syllables in English are of the *same* length; we, therefore, like the Greeks and Romans, must have long and short syllables. Which are they? how are they distinguished? Not as long and short; we never speak or think of them in that light; but as we disguise (even from ourselves) quantity under the name of accent, so we disguise long and short syllables under the name of accented and unaccented. There is, however, one very striking difference between our prosody and that of the ancients: in theirs the law of *position* prevailed throughout; and when a vowel stood before two consonants, it was, in most cases, at once known to be long: that law has no place in our prosody; we seem even to sport with it, making syllables, long by position, alternately long and short in the same word. The ancients naturally dwell, as we do, on the long syllables, and, as we do, passed rapidly over the short, which they could do with perfect ease, from the nature of those syllables in their languages, particularly from the terminations of their words being so frequently on a vowel, or a single consonant: but in ours, the terminations of all the participles of the present tense, a very numerous set, are on *ing*, and all of them unaccented, and therefore short: and in other words, a number of finals, equally unaccented, are on *act, ict, ex, int, ade, ense,* and many others of the same kind: these are often, in our language and versification, truly short syllables, and as such we pass over them as quickly as we can (practice giving great facility), till we come to an accented or long syllable. A Greek or a Roman would indeed have started at such trochees, iambi, and dactyls, (for such they are, in the very teeth of position), as heărĭng, rēlĭct, cōntrăct, ĭncĕnse, ĭncēnse, cōmplĕx, cŏmplaīn, līmĭtĭng, coūntĕrăct, cīrcŭmflĕx, frānkĭncĕnse, &c. Should any one doubt, whether such finals are really made short in our pronunciation, let him place an accent on *each* syllable of the dissyllables, and obey both the marks, and he will find the trochees and iambi changed into spondees; *cómpléx, incénse, cóntráct,* having the same quantity and cadence as *vast weight,* or *jam nunc;* and by the same process the dactyls changed into amphimacers, as *limitíng, círcumfléx, fránkincénse;* just as we do pronounce *disbeliéf, únconcérn'd.* This has been a long, but a necessary, preparation: I shall now apply it to the main object, which forms the next article.

Our system of pronouncing the two ancient languages.

THE system is founded on one general rule, very
strictly observed; that of laying our accent, or acute,
where the Romans laid their acute. They always laid
it on one syllable, and on one only, in every word not a
monosyllable; so we do ours: they laid it indifferently
on long and on short syllables; and we do as they did.
Now it is evident, that if we lay an accent which gives
length on any short syllable, we commit, each time
we do so, a direct and positive false quantity, and it is
obvious what numbers of them must proceed from this
source only: but there is another source of them not
less prolific. The spondee, bacchius, and antibacchius,
moērēns, sĕrēnōs, rēgīnă, have each two long syllables.
The *rule* commands us not to accent more than one,
the other therefore must remain unaccented and short;
in each word therefore we indirectly but necessarily
make one false quantity. The molossus has all the
three syllables long, as cōncīdēns; as we accent that in
the middle only, the first and last are short in spite of
position; and thus we make two false quantities in each
molossus. The choriambus has two long and two short
syllables, αῑγῐᾰλῷ: we lay our accent on one of the short
ones, and therefore make three false quantities in every
choriambus, one direct, and two indirect; when both sets
are added together, the list is enormous. The whole of
what I have said, or mean to say, rests on one fundamental maxim, the truth of which, in theory at least,
no one can dispute, " Salus metri suprema lex esto,"

there can be no metre with even a single false quantity; we often make two, not unfrequently three, in a single word; and in not a few hexameters, as many false quantities as there are feet. This is the undeniable consequence of reading by what is called *accent:* and were I to stop here, enough, more than enough, has surely been said to redeem the pledge I gave in the preface; for in what way is it possible to defend a system of reciting verses, by which the very essence of versification, *metre,* is destroyed? This however, though enough perhaps for the purpose of conviction, is not sufficient for that of feeling and impression: I therefore shall go on with the task I have undertaken, and to the best of my abilities shall trace the effects of the system in all its different bearings, and expose its striking deformities and ludicrous absurdities in every varied point of view in which I can contrive to place them; in the hope that what may slightly affect one set of readers, may strongly affect another.

I have stated the consequences of our being guided by the general rule of Latin accentuation: I shall now mention a particular rule by which we also are guided. Quintilian, in speaking of the difference between Greek and Latin accentuation, observes, that the Romans never laid an acute (as the Greeks often did) on any final syllable; that is, never raised the voice on any; the *quantity* of the syllable being totally independent of the accent, and either long or short, as the known rules of prosody and the structure of the verse might require; and he feelingly laments the vapid monotony occasioned by the Latin mode, compared with the flexible variety produced by that of the Greeks. In supposed conformity with this Latin rule, (which, by Quintilian's account of it, had better have been neglected altogether) we carefully avoid laying *our* acute on any Latin final, and consequently make every one of them short throughout the whole of that language without any exception, and with comparatively few exceptions throughout the Greek. This is what Quintilian could never have dreamed of; who indeed could dream of so gross a misconception of the Latin rule, and of so perverse a misapplication of it to quantity, by means of which the vapid monotony complained of is a mere trifle in comparison? no one who reflects at all upon the subject can help being aware of the injury which this strange *qui pro quo* must do to the Greek and Latin; yet, as every one is in the constant habit of doing it in practice, little if any feeling will be excited for the injured languages. The case is very different in our own, or in any modern language with which we are familiar; in *them* we most sensibly feel any false quantity; and if in the recitation of verses the long final of one of our iambi or anapæsts were to be shortened, we should at once *feel*, what under the same circumstances in Greek and Latin we do not even *perceive*, that the metre and rhythm were destroyed. On these accounts, before I proceed to what *is* done to the Greek and Latin, I shall begin by shewing what *would* be done to the English and Italian, were the *rule* applied to them, which it might be with just as much reason; and perhaps by exciting a strong and lively feeling in respect to the two modern languages, some part of it may be transferred to the two ancient. I will now request my English and Italian readers to consider what must be the necessary consequence of such an application; and first, in regard to variety.

The most fruitful source of variety in the sound and cadence of a language is the diversity of terminations; and one principal branch of diversity is a due proportion of long and short final syllables ; these, indeed, so evidently give relief to one another, and prevent the ear from being fatigued by a perpetual recurrence of syllables of the same length at the end of every word, that if we were to hear of a language in which all the final syllables were of one length, whether long or short, we should at once pronounce that the monotony must be insufferable : therefore, in this point of view only, the English and Italian languages would, by such a change, be injured beyond all endurance.

Connection is another most essential quality, without which variety would lose its greatest charms, and be little more than mere diversity. A due proportion of long syllables is highly necessary for the purpose of connection, whether we consider words as separate, or in combination. In the first case, they form resting-places for the voice, by means of which, when those places are happily disposed, especially in polysyllables, the whole may be blended together by an easy and harmonious articulation. In the second case, their peculiar use is at the end of words, as the voice is enabled to dwell on them, so as to blend and unite the word to which such a last syllable belongs, with the first of the succeeding word. On the other hand, feet with short finals, as trochees and dactyls, cannot blend with one another, each remains distinct and unconnected, as *arma, primus, ora, Tityre, tegmine, dulcia;* and it is probably owing to this obvious disconnection and monotony, that even two distinct dactyls in succession are rarely met with in hexameters, and never, as far as I have observed, three of them. Now the iambus and the anapæst (the one the reverse of the trochee, the other of the dactyl), by means of their long finals, do blend with one another; three iambi in succession are occasionally found at the end of the iambic verses, as "κατω θεων δικη," and it is evident that κατώ θεών, or θεών δική, form well connected compounds. In the same manner (though the poets were naturally sparing in the use of *any* three distinct feet in succession) we sometimes meet with three successive anapæsts, each a distinct word, in hexameters. As we shorten the very numerous long finals throughout the two ancient languages, by that alone all proportion between long and short syllables is obviously destroyed: nor does the mischief end here; for many other long syllables, in other parts of words (the cadence and character of the words themselves being totally altered), are, in consequence of shortening the final, likewise shortened; of which, and of all that has just been advanced, many striking examples will be given. The mischief would have been equally great, if we had taken it into our heads to lengthen all the *short* finals : their general characteristic is lightness and vivacity ; and in many verses they are used exclusively with the happiest effect : the characteristic of long finals (in the same general way of speaking) is firmness and dignity ; both of them, and a due proportion of each, are required for the perfection of language ; and when both are pronounced according to quantity, they give such constant and striking relief to one another, that we might apply to them, *mutatis mutandis,* what Gray says on a higher and more extensive subject,

> The hues of bliss more brightly glow,
> Chastised by sabler tints of woe ;
> And blended form with artful strife
> The strength and harmony of life.

Perspicuity is obviously a quality of the highest consequence. In most languages there are words composed of the same letters, which are distinguished from each other solely by a different length in a final syllable : in English this chiefly happens where a noun, either substantive or adjective, is to be distinguished from the verb ; as *présent presént, próduce prodúce, rébel rebél,* &c. and it is obvious, that if in such words the accent were to be uniformly laid on the first syllable, the clearness of the language would so far be injured ; but for the full extent and degree of such injury, we must look to the Italian. In that the long final in such a number of cases is the distinguishing mark, that if it were taken away, the whole construction of the language, its moods, tenses, persons, verbs, nouns, &c. would all be in total confusion. One or two instances will be sufficient. *A'mo* is *I love, amò he loved;* and thus, without any other difference but in the length of the last syllable, the same word is made to signify in the clearest manner a different tense and person. *Móri,* again, is *die,* in the imperative mood ; *morì, he died,* in the indicative perfect : here then is a difference of mood, as well as of tense and person. This short and clear method of distinguishing what requires the clearest discrimination, pervades the whole language ; but by the application of the *rule* it would be totally abolished. Every Englishman must feel from this statement, and evéry Italian still more strongly from the last part of it, that their respective languages would scarcely deserve the name, if so much bereaved of all that is most valuable in language itself; they will still more sensibly feel it by means of a few examples from their poets. The conversion that would most frequently take place in English and Italian dissyllables (there being no pyr-rhus, and few spondees) would be that of an iambus into a trochee. I shall therefore first give some English and Italian examples of such a conversion. Every reader of Milton knows that spirited line which con-cludes Satan's speech to his fallen companions,

Awake, arise, or be for ever fall'n.

And those who may not have reflected how much the spirit and energy (not to mention the metre and

c 2

rhythm) depend on the two iambi at the beginning, will be fully sensible of it when they read,

> A'wăke, a'rĭse, or be for ever fall'n.

The same conversion, though it cannot well be more striking, is perhaps more ludicrous in the opening of one of Gray's odes, as the line begins and ends with the iambus:

> A'wake Æolian lyre, a'wake.

Or in Macbeth:

> Lay on, Māc'dŭff,
> And damn'd be he that first cries hold, e'noŭgh.

How would an Italian, and an admirer of Dante, start and cry out, if he were to hear,

> Vuolsi cósi cóla dove si puote;

or, in another style,

> A'mŏr che a nullo amato ā'măr perdona;

though he constantly accents ă'mōr, when an iambus in Latin, in the same manner. Thus far, although metre, rhythm, and expression are destroyed, and though the falsely accented words are in fact no words at all, and have no meaning, yet they have not a false one; but in many Italian lines the change of accent, in addition to all the rest, changes the tense, the person, and the mood, in some of the verbs. Thus in that noble line in Dante's Ugolino,

> Che del futuro mi squarciò 'l velame,

squār′ciŏ would be *I tear* in the present, instead of *tore* in the perfect; and as to the rhythm, it would be changed from the heroic into a kind of sing-song, divided into two parts:

Che del futuro | mi squār′ciŏ 'l velame.

Another most impressive line in the same striking part would be completely spoilt:

Ed io sēn′tĭ chīávăr l'uscio di sotto.

Sē′ntĭ is the second person of the indicative present, or the first of the imperative, instead of the first of the indicative perfect. As to chīávăr, it may be a sort of *lingua franca* of any mood, tense, or person; and Ugolino, instead of *I heard* (and we know how alarming a sound), appears to say, in the mixture of false Italian and *patois*, " and I—listen—lock the door below." The rhythm is hardly less injured than the sense: the two iambi, which give such strength to the expression, give equal strength and equal variety (placed as they are between the trochees ī′ŏ and l'ūsciŏ) to the rhythm: by shortening the long finals, all this would be destroyed, and there would be five almost successive trochees in the same line,

Ed ī′o sēn′tĭ chīávăr l'ū′sciŏ di sōt′tŏ.

These are all the quotations from the two modern languages that I shall give for the present. I have endeavoured to shew in the strongest light, and from the most striking examples, what would be the effects of the *rule* upon them; though, as I am bound to shew that those effects are still more injurious to the ancient, I have increased the difficulty of my engagement.

We are so habituated to the exclusive use of short finals in Greek and Latin, nay, are so well satisfied and pleased with their effect, that we shall not easily be brought to allow of their being altogether injurious, or at least at all in the same degree as, from the examples just given, they evidently would be in the English and the Italian: most of my readers therefore will be surprised at the assertion in the following article. *The injury, however grievous and extensive, that would be done to the English and Italian languages, were every long final syllable throughout the whole of them made short, would be by many degrees less grievous and less extensive than that which is actually done to the Greek and Latin by shortening those syllables.* It seems fair to conclude, that in such cases the degree of injury will be very much in proportion to the number of long finals: now, I believe, it will be found, that in a given number of lines taken from any part of Homer and Virgil, there will be at least twice, perhaps nearly thrice, as many long finals as in the same number of lines taken in the same manner from Milton, Dryden, Ariosto, and Tasso; and this without taking into the account the concluding syllables of the hexameter, though a large portion of them might very fairly be counted, as being long in all situations. In the Greek and Latin verses that will hereafter be quoted, the numerous long finals will strike the reader from their being uniformly shortened in consequence of the *rule*, and from their being always marked as short: but before I proceed to any examples, it may be a useful, if not a necessary preparation, to take a view of the feet most commonly used in the ancient metres, and to shew how many of them are affected by the *rule*; and afterwards to point out the manner in which, according to my notions, they ought to be pronounced.

Dissyllabic feet.

The trochee, as ār'dĕt, we very properly accent on the first syllable, which therefore is pronounced long, and the last short. The iambus, as ă'māns, as improperly on the same syllable, as we exactly reverse its true quantity, and commit two false quantities in every one of them. By the same mode of accenting, we make one false quantity in every spondee, as ā'mēns, shortening the last syllable; and one on every pyrrhic, as ă'mŏr, by lengthening the first; and thus all the four dissyllabic feet are reduced to a single one—the trochee.

Trisyllabic feet.

The dactyl, which is a trochee with an additional short syllable at the end, as rē'gĭbŭs, we very properly accent, as we do the trochee, on the first. The anapæst (an iambus with the same addition at the beginning), as rē'dŭcēs, we as improperly accent on the first, reversing, as in the iambus, the true quantity, and making two false quantities. The amphimacer, as rē'gĭōs, we likewise accent on the first; and by shortening the last make one false quantity: each of these feet thus loses its own character, and becomes a dactyl. The molossus (a spondee with an additional long syllable), as constric'tōs, we do not accent, like the spondee, on the first, but on the second, and therefore do not change it into a dactyl, but into an amphibrachys. The bacchius, as ărīs'tās, and the antibacchius, as rē-gī'nă, by the same mode of accenting (though the change is less striking than in many of the others), are also turned into the amphibrachys. By such means these ten feet, on the skilful arrangement and intermixture of which, each having its distinct and appropriate character, the exactness of metre, the varied harmony of rhythm, and the various modes of expression and of imitative harmony so much depend, are reduced to three, the trochee, the dactyl, and the amphibrachys.

Pronunciation of the ancient feet according to quantity.

WE have just seen in what manner the *rule* has curtailed the number of the ancient feet; and yet, with the few that are left us, we fancy ourselves reciting ancient poetry in all its metres, with the most enchanting rhythm and varied harmony! What if some capricious tyrant, a Nero or a Caligula, had ordered two thirds of the strings to be cut off here and there from a lyre, and had then commanded the poor musician to play some of his favourite pieces, and to give them the same variety and effect as when the strings were complete! He would then have done just what that mis-

chievous tyrant the *Rule* has done in regard to the
ancient languages; and our present performance, with
less than a third of the ancient feet, is very much
what in such a case the musician's must have been. I
am very anxious that we should restore those feet to
their full complement, the preliminary step being of
course the restoration of the true quantity: and the
only difficulty—by no means a slight one—seems to be
that of inspiring an earnest wish to restore it, from an
entire conviction of the vast improvement which would
take place, in every point of view, throughout the ancient languages. The main object would then indeed
be gained, and every thing else, sooner or later, must
follow; but at present, from what I have heard in
conversation, and met with in writings, on the subject,
I am persuaded, that although we are in all cases perfectly acquainted with quantity by the eye, yet we are
in many quite unacquainted with it by the ear. I have,
for instance, often heard it maintained, that by laying
an accent on the first syllable of a Latin spondee, as
moérens, we do not make the unaccented syllable shorter
than the accented[c]; but I think it will be felt that we

[c] A writer of high reputation, Mr. Harris, the author of Hermes, has
given the word *fountains* as an example of a true spondee in English, as in

Fountains, and ye that warble as ye flow.

I believe the word to be not less truly a trochee than most of those in our
language, as I think will clearly be shewn by a reference to another language and pronunciation. Let a Frenchman repeat the line, and he will
naturally pronounce the first word like *fontaines,*

Fŏúntaĭ'ns, and ye that warble as ye flow,

do make it long, when, by an additional syllable, it
ceases to be a final; for upon comparing the sound in
such cases with that of the word when single, the difference in length will clearly be perceived.

The addition I allude to, that of a *que* or a *ne* to any
Latin word, will in most cases serve as a test and a
guide; and in the following way : if we find that we
pronounce the word exactly in the same manner without the enclitic as with it, we are right; if differently,
wrong. Thus we say ármaque and árma exactly the
same with or without the *que;* as also solútaque and
solúta : but though we say sĕnē'xquĕ we say sē'nĕx,
moērē'nsquĕ but moē'rĕns, lăpĭdē'squĕ but lā'pĭdĕs, cōn-
strīctō'squĕ but cŏnstrī'ctŏs, īngĕnī'quĕ but ī'ngĕnĭ, mēr-
cātōrē'squĕ but mērcătōrĕs, īngĕmĭnā'ntquĕ but īngē'-

---

and will consequently make it a true spondee, and a standard (as *fontaines*
is) for the quantity of that foot. Mr. Harris may have been led into this
error (for such I presume it is) by that which had led many writers into
similar errors, a reference to ancient prosody; and certainly in any Greek
or Latin word a diphthong followed by two consonants would have been a
long syllable ; but with us the law of position has no force, and we are used
to leap over much stronger barriers. In this too, as in so many cases, we
vary in the pronunciation of the same letters, and sound *tains* nearly as we
do *tens*, passing over the vowels to the consonants, and not dwelling on
them ; and by such means have little difficulty in shortening the unaccented
syllable of the iambus *maintáins;* we rest on the vowels, giving to them the
sound which they commonly have in English, that of a long *a,* and much
the same with *ai* in *fontaines.* Here then the three feet are plainly discri-
minated : *fountains* is a trochee, *maintains* (in which we sound the first
syllable nearly like *men*) an iambus, and *fontaines* a spondee. Lay an
accent on the last as well as on the first of *fóuntáins,* and on the first as well
as on the last of *máintáins,* and all the three words are true spondees, and
equally so : this sort of analysis will apply to all cases of a similar kind.

mĭnănt. It is thus that the enclitic serves as a test: as a guide, the rule for applying it (a very simple one, and already indicated) is, that we should pronounce such words without the *que* exactly as we pronounced them with it.

It may perhaps be said, that on all such occasions we are observing throughout the Latin rules of accentuation; not merely as to the syllable on which we are to avoid laying the acute, but as to that on which we are to lay it; for whenever an enclitic was added, the Romans transferred the acute from the syllable on which it had been laid to that which, by the addition, became the penultima, as sénex senéxque, lápides lapidésque, constríctos constrictósque. It is very true, and we are quite right on such occasions in laying our accent where they laid theirs; not *because* they laid it there, but because the syllable is long, and our accent obliges us to pronounce it so. I believe that the enclitic will, in most cases, answer the purpose I have mentioned; but the most natural and ready guides, as far as they can be had, and as far as we can be sure of their accuracy, are the same feet in our own languages, and there are some such in English, and many more in Italian.

English and Italian feet that correspond with those in Greek and Latin.

THE trochee in Italian is a perfect standard for the pronunciation of the ancient foot, which (as the rule does not interfere, as it does in some of the others) the

Italian pronounces in perfection. Our English trochees, under which denomination I include all dissyllables accented on the first syllable, may be divided into two classes, the one more imperfect than the other, and neither of them having the perfection of the Italian : the cause of this difference between the two, and between them both and the Italian, may throw some light on this part of the subject. We have an unfortunate propensity in our language, to pass over the vowel to the consonant in the first syllables of words, which thence, *although* accented, are comparatively short; as *véry, bánish;* and it makes no difference, position having no force, whether the consonant be doubled; as we pronounce *mérry* and *bánner* just in the same way, not separating the two consonants, but sounding them as if only a single one. In many trochees we stop on the vowel; as *wáry, báneful,* and the syllables are manifestly longer than in the others : there are also trochees equally long with the last, where we do pass to a consonant, but followed by another of a different kind; which therefore we are obliged to separate, and distinguish from each other, as *ar'my.*

[d] Now the Italians never pass over the vowel to a

[d] The difference of length, as has just been mentioned, so regularly and uniformly takes place, from the cause which has been assigned, that our accented syllables might very properly be divided into two distinct classes of short and long, or of long and short accents. In Johnson's Dictionary the accentual mark is in all cases placed immediately after the vowel, as présent, préfect, préssingly, ármy, ármament ; and this merely shews that they are all accented on the first syllable, and nothing further : now, in my

single consonant; and when they pass over it to two of the same kind, they separate them in pronunciation, so that the sound of each is distinctly heard: thus in the words *cer'ri* and *fer'ri* they separate the consonants, and sound each *r*; and in so doing, of course give greater length and effect to the first syllable. We, in pronouncing nearly the same words in sound, as *cher'y*, *ferr'y*, give no more length or distinction to the double *r* than if it had been single. The Italian manner of pronouncing the trochee is therefore, in all respects, the true model for our imitation [e].

Our English iambi I hold to be not less perfect than the Italian, and more so they could not be; and had it not been for the accentual system, we and the Italians should both of us naturally have pronounced the ancient iambi as we do our own; for it is most unnatural to do otherwise. What makes the case still stronger, and shews in the most glaring light our submissive

mind, it would be very useful, especially to foreigners, if the difference were to be indicated, as it might so easily be, by the position of the accentual mark; if, for instance, it were always to be placed immediately after the vowel, when we stop upon it, as préfect, precédency; after the consonant, when we pass on to it, as in pres'ent and armip'otent; after both consonants, when they are the same in form and sound, as press'ingly; and between both, when different in sound, and therefore detached, as ac'cent, ab'sent. This method would at once indicate the varying length of our accented syllables, and its cause.

[e] The Italian trochees, as they are much more perfect than ours in reality, so they likewise are in appearance. The greater part of them end on a vowel, whereas a very great part of ours end on two consonants, for all our dissyllabic participles of the present tense end on two consonants, by no means favourable to rapid articulation.

obedience to the *rule*, is, that there are several iambi in English, which very exactly correspond in sound, and some of them letter for letter, with others in Greek and Latin; yet though we lay the accent in all ours on the last, we lay it on the first in the ancient ones. We have in English the words abýss, agó, agaín, afár, jocóse, moráss, refér, which in Greek and Latin we change into ā′bis, ἄ′γῶ, ā′gŏ, ἄ′γĕν, ἄ′φᾰρ, jō′cŏs, mō′răs, rē′fĕr. In Italian there is a long list of iambi completely Latin words: amòr, furòr, dolòr, colòr, ferì, cavò, &c. &c. all these in Latin, when the first four are iambi by position (and it is nearly as wrong when they are pyrrhics), the Italians, in direct contradiction to their own constant habits, as well as to the ancient prosody, force themselves to pronounce ámor, fúror, dólor, &c. With regard to the true pronunciation of the ancient iambus there can be no doubt or difficulty; we have perfect examples in both languages, and have only to follow them.

The spondee is not congenial to our language, and not múch more so to the Italian. The word most commonly proposed as an English spondee (not certainly a very English one) is *amen*; and when distinctly pronounced on solemn occasions, nearly an equal length is given to each of the syllables. *Finite* has also been mentioned; but our habits always incline us, on common occasions, to accent one of the syllables [f]. In

---

[f] Johnson accents *amén* on the last, and that is the accent which in English we are inclined to; yet in Greek the *rule* forces us, in spite of the *eta* in the last syllable, to accent it on the first, as in ἀμὴν λέγω ὑμῖν, where

Italian, as it seems to me, there are many more spondees than in English, and their quantity more fixed;
though all of them are accented on the last syllable
only. I conceive the word *virtù* to be so near a true
spondee, that it might very well serve as a general
standard for that foot, and would particularly correct
the trochaic pronunciation of vĭ'rtŭs; and that *virtù* is
not an iambus will at once be perceived by comparing
it with an undoubted one, as *vedèr;* such words too as
fautòr, testè, beltà, seem to be of the same kind; as
likewise the infinitives, and the preterperfects in the
third person singular of many verbs, the first syllables
of which could not well be made short, as *giostràr,
sforzàr, giostrò,* &c. &c. Most of these are contracted
from longer words, as *virtute, beltade, giostrare,* &c.
and luckily, I may say, have retained, when dissyllables, the accent on the penultima; for such contracted
nouns and verbs furnish the chief part of the long finals
in the Italian language; without them it would have
been originally formed with almost the same degree of

we make all the dissyllables equally trochees, and, as is often the case,
destroy the sense with the quantity; and instead of λἴγῶ, *I say,* make it in
pronunciation ληγω, *I cease.* *Finite* is accented by Johnson (but he gives
no example from poetry) on the first: it seems rather doubtful on which of
the two syllables we are most disposed to lay the accent; but I conceive
that he must be wrong in placing it on the same syllable in *finitely,* as we
certainly do not pronounce it, as the accent indicates, fīnĭtelÿ. *Finite* does
not occur in Shakespear, and only once in Milton:

> For anger's sake, finite to infinite:

and in that part of the verse may be a trochee, a spondee, or an iambus.
The word *July* is perhaps the best instance of a spondee in English.

monotony in so very essential a respect as that to which the *rule* has reduced the ancient languages. These contractions, then, which have given to the Italian such a number of perfect iambi, have also given it a certain number of spondees, which may very well serve as standards for the pronunciation of that foot.

The pyrrhic is the only one among these feet, for which, according to my notions, there is no true standard, either in English or Italian; for as all our words of two syllables are accented on the one or the other, and as both syllables in the pyrrhic are equally short, no such accent can properly be laid on either. In this case recourse cannot be had to the enclitic; for when the pyrrhic ends on a consonant, as cĕlĕr, *que* immediately turns it into an iambus, and the whole into an amphibrachys, cĕlērquĕ: an expedient, however, of a similar kind, which I shall soon have occasion to propose, will answer the same purpose. We accent the pyrrhic, like every other ancient dissyllable, on the first, and make it a trochee; on the other hand, were we to accent it on the last, it would be an iambus: both are in fact equally wrong; but whenever the pyrrhic is to be pronounced as a single independent word, or is to be joined to a preceding long syllable as the end of a dactyl, it appears to have more affinity with the iambus than with the trochee: all this will, I trust, be made clear by the following example. We say *cólor*, but not *discólor;* for it would be called, what it so truly is, a false quantity: but again, at the beginning of an hexameter, we say *Qui cólor*, which, though just as much a false quantity as the other, is not called one, because it is sanctioned by the *rule*. In this case, then, an additional syllable at the *beginning* of a word is as safe a guide as a *que* at the *end* of them in the other cases : we have only to pronounce *discolor* as usual, and then *color* without the *dis*, exactly as we had done with it, and *Qui color* the same[g]. By this method, though we have no standards for pyrrhics in our own language, the true sound of it is pointed out in a way that can hardly fail to be satisfactory, that is, from our own pronunciation of the foot itself, though somewhat in disguise.

We have many dactyls in English, none of them quite perfect, and most of them very imperfect ; and our pronunciation of the ancient dactyls is much more imperfect than that of the trochees. It so happens, that in them we seldom pass over a vowel to a *single*

---

[g] The mark, which is of a negative kind, is intended to warn the reader not to lay *any* accent on the first syllable, as that would check the progress, *ipso in limine*, of this rapid foot; and likewise to indicate that he is to give the slightest possible touch, and no more than is necessary for articulation, to the last : and if he passes quickly over one to the other, and quits the last almost as soon as he has touched upon it, he will give to the whole that peculiar lightness, the true characteristic of the pyrrhic, which distinguishes it from the other ancient dissyllabic feet, and of which I believe there is scarcely an example in any modern dissyllable. The iambus and the trochee are both of them rapid feet ; and that they were considered as such by the ancients, appears from the etymology of the one, and the descriptions given of the other but the etymology of the pyrrhic from the element of. fire, seems to indicate, that it was not only fiery footed, but that it had also the lightness of flame : and I hope to shew, by different examples from the poets, how much we ought to attend, in the pronunciation of it, to so characteristic a distinction.

consonant, whereas we perpetually do so in the dactyls, and often in some of the oblique cases of the very same noun: thus we say ómen, but om'ine, (and in this instance it is the same in English, omen, ominous,) réges, but reg'ibus; we also say Títe, but Tit'yre. This the Italians never do; and their pronunciation of the dactyl, when a separate word, is a perfect standard, both in their own and the ancient languages.

The pronunciation of the anapæst, like that of iambus, to which it bears so much affinity, is equally exact both in English and Italian. In the ancient languages we have only to get rid of the *rule*, and instead of laying the accent on the first syllable in such words as rĕ'fĕrēs, to lay it on the last, as in refereés and referì.

We have seen that in English, spondees are very rare; and that they are much less so in Italian, though to that language they are not congenial, as they are to those of the ancients: the same habits which indispose us to give an equal length to two long syllables, operate more strongly in regard to three; and accordingly, as far as I have observed, there is no true molossus in English. In Italian, as it appears to me, such words as *destruttòr, rinforzàr*, and others of the same kind, have nearly an equal length on each of the syllables; and if the middle one should be rather the shortest, yet the word altogether will not less effectually tend to correct the most prominent fault in the usual pronunciation of the molossus; that of making the middle syllable the *only* long one. This will clearly be seen, by substituting an Italian spondee and molossus for those feet accented in the usual manner in the Latin, as, instead of *Vírtus, torméntum, Virtù, tormentàr*. These give, as nearly as one could desire, the right quantity and cadence of two such feet at the beginning of an hexameter, as in Horace's "Majus tormentum," and therefore may very well serve as standards.

The amphimacer, as *ingeni*, (a foot not admissible in the hexameter, but in constant use in many other metres) is common enough both in English and Italian, as *dísbeliéf, giudicàr*.

The choriambus, ĭngĕmĭnānt, is not common in English; as all the words which have been adopted from the ancient choriambi (many of them the most poetical in our language) are accented, like the originals, on the second syllable, as *Elýsian, nectáreous, ambrósial*, &c. There are few of English growth; such adopted words, however, as *arquebusade, chandanagore*, are very true choriambi. The Italians, like ourselves, have accented most of the adopted choriambi on the second syllable, as *nettáreo, contínuo*, &c. but from the lucky circumstance already mentioned, of their contracted nouns and verbs, they have many examples of this beautiful foot, as *continuò, imperadòr, incoronàr*, and the ancient choriambi ought evidently to be pronounced in the same manner.

The dispondee it would be vain to look for in English; in Italian there are some words, as *discomfortàr*, which, though not exact enough for standards, would serve to correct our pronunciation of εὔρυκρείων and mēr'cătŏ'rĕs. Here then, I may venture to say, are many perfect standards, either in English or in Italian, for the pronunciation of some of the principal metrical feet used in ancient versification, together with others, which, though imperfect, answer nearly the same purpose, and in aid of these last, and alone sufficient for every purpose but one, the test and guidance of the enclitic: and lastly, where the enclitic fails, and where, as we pronounce the words, there is no dissyllabic standard in any language, we may ascertain the true sound and cadence of the pyrrhic by means of a preceding long syllable in compounds. These different modes have the same result; the cadences being always in perfect accord with one another, and with those which must have been given by the ancients in their recitation: unless we suppose, what no one who makes use of his reason can suppose, that the Greek and Latin poets constructed their verses by one set of rules, and recited them by another of a totally different kind. This is what we manifestly, nay avowedly, do: and what is our plea? I never heard but one, which has already been mentioned, namely, that we lay our accent where the Romans laid theirs; and this, as I trust has been fully shewn, is a mere juggle of words, the modern sense of accent having no relation to that of the ancient; the plea therefore is null and void. If indeed it could be shewn that some grammarian of high authority has clearly and unequivocally stated that the ancients, in the recitation of verses, uniformly lengthened every acuted syllable, however short by the structure of the verse, and shortened every unaccented one, however long, our plea and our practice would acquire a very strong, and a most unexpected support: were it possible that such a passage could be discovered, and triumphantly placed before my eyes, what could I say? I should not say, like the person who saw a notorious miser give a louis d'or to a charity, " si je ne l'avois pas vu, je ne l'aurois jamais cru," but like Fontenelle, "moi qui l'ai vu, je n'y crois pas." It might be difficult to give such direct and positive proof that the ancients did pronounce those syllables short which we pronounce long, and vice versa, so as to silence all cavils; but the degree of probability on one side amounts almost, if not quite, to a certainty, and the improbability on the other, as nearly to an impossibility. Luckily however we have, on the authority of the best grammarians, to whom I most readily give my full belief, the undoubted guide which the ancients followed in their recitation. It will form the title of the next article.

Ictus Metricus, Arsis, and Thesis.

TILL within these few years I scarcely knew any thing more of these terms than the terms themselves, and therefore for the sake of those who may know no more of them than I did, a short explanation seems to be required; should it contain any inaccuracies, I may hope some of my learned readers will correct them. It likewise seems a necessary preparation for what I shall have to advance respecting the great use and advantage of the Ictus, &c. as the surest and most approved guide in recitation, and as an effectual correction of our most offensive sins against quantity, metre, and rhythm. The Ictus metricus, as its name indicates, is a stroke or stress given to certain syllables in metrical compositions ; in the hexameter, to which for the present I shall chiefly confine myself, it is always on the first of each foot, and therefore always on the first syllable at the beginning of each verse, and on the last but one at the end of it ; with regard to the arsis and thesis, Bentley calls that time where the ictus is, *the arsis*; those times where the ictus is not, *the thesis*: and Hermann, though he observes that other writers have thought differently, says, after giving his reasons for so doing, " quare maluimus usum a Bentleio probatum servare." Bentley's opinion, sanctioned by Hermann, is as high as authority can well go[h]. By the terms *arsis* and *thesis* the ancients seem merely to have signified their mode of keeping and marking metrical time, much in the same way that a musician marks or *beats* musical time; they raised up, as the word implies, the hand or the foot on *arsis ;* and, as the other word denotes, put it down on *thesis ;* and this regular process went through each verse, as, in the other case, throughout each bar. The ictus was always on a long syllable; and length was so absolutely required, that where a vowel or a syllable was on other occasions short, the ictus had the power of lengthening

[h] A learned writer in the Edinburgh Review, however, " is inclined to suspect that the *arsis* and *thesis* refer rather to the elevation and depression of the foot in dancing, than to the pulsation of the tibicen." vol. xviii. p. 183.

it, as in the well known instances of Αρες Αρες, of Διά μεν ασπιδος, of Επειδη τονδ' ανδρα, and others in the middle of verses. I shall here suggest to the reader's notice, the analogy which in several respects subsists between the ictus and our accent; both of them are always on a long syllable; both have the power, just mentioned, of lengthening short syllables; and both give an emphasis to the syllable on which they are laid: there is, however, one most essential difference between them, which should be carefully kept in mind: the ictus acts solely upon the syllable on which it is laid; it does not affect the others, which keep their usual quantity; whereas our accent (and I believe the same may in a great degree be said of the Italian) acts equally by its presence and its absence; not only lengthening the accented syllable, but shortening (except in some cases of polysyllables) the unaccented. Supposing us therefore to adopt in practice, what there is such strong and obvious reason for adopting, the ancient guide in recitation, there might be some danger of considering the ictus in the same light as the accent, and of shortening, from the effect of habit in the other case, the syllables on which it was not laid. This will be best explained by an example; but as the example will be the first *entire* ancient verse that I shall have quoted, it will be necessary to explain the manner in which I shall mark it, and the purpose for which it will be so marked, as I shall throughout these pages mark in the same way almost all the lines I shall have occasion to quote. *Above* the line then I shall place the accentual mark immediately after the syllables upon which we lay our accent in recitation, and shall also place *over* those same accented syllables (whether really long or short) the ancient mark of long ; and over all the unaccented syllables (whatever may be their real quantity) the mark of short. Those readers (much the most numerous, I believe, of the general mass of them), who have never thought of accent as identified with quantity, but as something quite distinct from it, will be not a little startled at seeing the mark of short over diphthongs, etas, and omegas, over vowels followed by two, and even three, consonants ; and, on the other hand, the mark of long over epsilons, omicrons, and other vowels as notoriously short; they will scarcely be brought to believe, for it is scarcely credible, that they have all their lives been unconsciously breaking all the laws of metre and prosody, deceived and hood-winked by that misleading term *accent*. They will very naturally be led to suspect me of having committed some gross error in such an application of the ancient marks ; I will venture to say, however, that if they will obey them, and recite the verses exactly by their guidance, they will find themselves reciting them pre-cisely in their usual manner. These will be the marks *above* the line; *below* it I shall constantly place a stroke (the same as the mark of long) *under* every syllable that receives the ictus ; and likewise occasionally, the little mark by which I have indicated the right pro-nunciation of the pyrrhic : this I shall also place *under* the syllable, and *below* the line, not to interfere with the marks above it. The arrangement will enable the reader at one view to compare the two modes of recitation, and the position of the different marks, and to observe where they vary from, or coincide with, one another.

Spĕctā'tŭm vē'nĭŭnt vē'nĭŭnt spĕctēn'tŭr ŭt ĭ'psaĕ.

In this example (a mild one compared with many that will be given) the line in our mode begins with a bastard amphibrach, a foot, were it a true one, inadmissible in that place; then comes a spurious dactyl, followed by another of the same kind; and that by another amphibrach equally inadmissible where it stands. The concluding dissyllable we make a trochee, pronouncing it like *ipse*. Dactyls and spondees are the only legitimate feet, into one of which all others that may be introduced must be resolvable; as we pronounce the line, there is no spondee, and till you come to the adonic[1], no dactyl: we are however well pleased and satisfied with the rhythm, though it neither belongs to the hexameter, nor to any other metre. Now if we follow the guidance of the ictus, we *must* give the due length to four long syllables, which we shorten in our mode, and among them to the last syllable of the second *veniunt*, where the vowel is followed by two consonants in the same word, and by

---

[1] I have made use of this word to signify the dactyl and spondee, however formed, at the end of the hexameter; and shall continue so to employ it as a convenient, though perhaps not an accurate, term.

two others in the next; and if we give the due length
and stress to the syllables on which the ictus is laid,
and in regard to the others, observe, as we are bound
to do, the known rules of prosody, we shall have six
legitimate feet, three spondees, and three dactyls, and
the metre and the rhythm will both of them be perfect.
But although upon this, as on every occasion, we are
bound to observe the rules of prosody, yet, as I have
already hinted, we are not unlikely, from our old accentual habits, to shorten any long syllables upon which
the ictus is *not* laid, and should then pronounce the line
in question :

Spēctătūm vĕnĭūnt vĕnĭūnt spĕctēntŭr ŭt īp'saĕ.

This would be very perverse and unexcusable, and
would obviously injure the metre, yet would comparatively but slightly affect the rhythm; the general flow
and hexametrical character of which is in a great degree
secured by the ictus. My object in mentioning this
circumstance is not, most assuredly, to sanction or
excuse any breach of quantity under any pretence, but
to point out the extensive use and advantage of adopting the ictus, which, at the same time that it completely
corrects our grossest and most offensive errors, would
soften the effect of any careless inaccuracies. Among
the various advantages of adopting the ictus, perhaps
the greatest use of all, is, that it would force us to give
the due length and stress, where we now never give
them, to the long finals; and, in consequence of so

doing, the true cadence and spirit to the iambi, anapæsts, and choriambi; and as in these last there is
always a double ictus, the stroke on the first would
drive the voice over the two short middle syllables to
the long final, and would give its genuine character to
that noble foot, as Ἠϊονες, and the same where there is a
preceding short syllable, as ερευγομενης, and again to
words with a double anapæst, as νεφεληγερετα Ζευς: in
all these not only the right quantity and rhythm are
restored, but euphony with ease and distinctness of
articulation. These, and other circumstances relative
to the ictus, will be frequently pressed upon the reader's
attention by the quotations: what has been said seems
quite sufficient for explanation and preparation. I shall
add however a line from Terentianus Maurus, very
much in favour of what I have advanced; for in speaking of the ictus metricus, and of the manner in which
ancient recitation was guided by that and by the arsis
and thesis, he says,

> Quicquid at his discrepabit absonum reddet melos.

Ambiguity.

In this particular point the Italian would be more
injured than the Greek, or perhaps than the Latin;
although these last, especially the Latin, are injured in
no small degree, as an example or two will shew. In
the following line, in the third book of the Iliad, Homer
describes the south wind (a very proper agent on such

an occasion) diffusing a mist over the summit of the mountain :

Ήΰτ' ορέός κορυφῆσι Νοτός κατεχεύεν ομίχλην.

As we accent the line a less proper agent is introduced.

Ήΰτ' ό'ρἒός κὅρΰφῆσῐ Νό'τὅς κἄτἒχεῦἒν ὅμῐ'χλην.

Νῶτος (for the only difference between the omicron and the omega, both being originally *o*, is the length) signifies the back of a man, or rather of an animal, which indeed at times emits a good deal of warm vapour, but not quite on so extensive a scale. There are many other dissyllables, both nouns and verbs, in which, ancient accent being now a dead letter, the only distinction is the long or the short vowel on the first syllables, as βρωτος βροτος, ληγω λεγω, ηχω εχω, γηρας γερας. We make no such distinction; and as we pronounce the last of these words, Achilles would have appeared to an ancient Greek, very plainly, however absurdly, to say to Agamemnon, " you threaten to take away my old age from me :"

Και δη μοι γῆρας αυτος αφαιρησεσθαι απειλεις.

A few lines farther on, the old Greek would have been completely puzzled by the addition of one of the verbs :

Ου γαρ σοι ποτε ισον ἔχῶ γἔρἄς :

and would only have been able to make out something very incongruous about sound and old age.

In Latin the moods, tenses, and persons, in many of the verbs, are distinguished, as in Italian, by the different length of the first or of the last syllable; in both a false quantity or accent turns sense into nonsense, as in a well known line in Ovid's Epistles. Penelope says to Ulysses, Do not write to me, but come yourself, " ipse veni;" as we accent the last word,

Nil mihi rescribas, attamen ipse véni,

the sense is nobly confounded; for the literal meaning is, " Do not write to me, but I am come myself;" and is a match for any change of mood, tense, and person, in Italian [k].

Besides the verbs I have alluded to, there are a number of nouns, both substantive and adjective, which are distinguished from each other solely by difference of quantity; and there is one set of them particularly (including a verb) so alike, yet with so many different meanings, that the most exact observance of their quantity cannot guard against some degree of ambiguity. Mālūm is an apple; mălūm, an evil; mālō, I prefer; mălō in the dative, bad; mālă, apples or a cheek; mălă, evils or bad; mālŭs, a mast; mălŭs, bad; and so they go on through cases and tenses: here are all the four dissyllabic feet; and if, when each has its appropriate sound and quantity, ambiguity cannot entirely be avoided, what must be the case when verbs,

[k] To suit the speaker it ought to be *ipsa*: but where there is so much confusion, the wrong sex is only a small addition.

substantives, and adjectives, however different in meaning and in quantity, all appear in the shape of trochees?

One difference between the Greek and Latin, respecting these dissyllabic feet, it is right to mention: in the Greek, while a living language, many of them were distinguished by a diversity in the accent, as well as in the quantity, νῶτος and νότος, γῆρας and γέρας, though even then a right accent with a wrong quantity would have been rather a lame distinction; but in Latin, dissyllables were generally, if not always, acuted on the first; and consequently, in regard to accent, exactly alike. We therefore must come to one of these two conclusions; either that the Romans, in such words as vēnī vĕnī, fūgĭt fŭgĭt, vēlīs vĕlīs, cănō cānō, did pronounce the syllables according to their true quantity; or, on the other hand, that in every one of them they pronounced the first (as being acuted) long, and the last short, and consequently made no distinction whatever, when the clearest distinction was so peculiarly required. The first conclusion accords with the structure of all their verses, and the known rules of their prosody; the second involves so manifest an absurdity, that if there were no other argument against the system altogether, this would, in my mind, be decisive.

Cæsura.

THE cæsura, as the word indicates, cuts or divides the verse; it forms a resting-place for the voice, and seems best to answer that and every other purpose,

when divisions are nearly equal; when it falls on a long
final; and when there is a pause in the sense; as in
μηνιν αειδε θεα, Æneadum genetrix, arma virumque cano.
It is certainly quite a sufficient reason for pronouncing
any syllable long, that it is so by the common rules of
prosody; but in this case the additional reasons, though
not required, are singularly striking; the cæsura is a
resting-place for the voice, which cannot have complete
rest except on a concluding syllable; and length is in
such cases so much required, that the cæsura is considered as having the power of making such syllables
long, though they should usually be short; and the
ictus, which has the same power to a wider extent,
generally, if not always, on such occasions, falls on the
same syllable. With these cogent reasons, added to
authority, position, diphthongs, &c. a syllable might
think its length perfectly secured; but our single rule
is too strong, far too strong, for them all; it commands
us to shorten all long finals (with a few exceptions in
Greek), wherever they may be found: and this despotic
order, like Turkish slaves, we blindly obey. The
extent of the massacre throughout the two languages is
beyond calculation; but we may form some idea of it
by what takes place on the one point in question. Of
the first hundred lines in the Georgics, about ninety
have the cæsura on long finals, and it is nearly the same
in the first hundred of the Æneid; therefore, supposing
this to be nearly the general proportion, seven thousand
cæsuras, at a moderate computation, will, in consequence
of our rule, be murdered in Virgil's works alone; and

we may imagine what would be the sum total, were the other numerous Latin poets considered in the same manner. In Greek—at least in the Homeric poems—the case is strikingly different. In the Iliad the proportion between cæsuras on long finals and the others seems to be nearly equal, though in favour of the *others;* in the Odyssey (judging in each poem from the first hundred lines in the two first books) much more so: still in the course of twice twenty-four books the number is considerable. It is again prodigiously augmented by the numerous pentameters, the first hemistich of which has always a marked cæsura, and almost always on a long final. Do we then *never* rest upon the cæsura? never give it its due length? we sometimes do, but only when it falls on a monosyllable, as in a line often quoted:

Et cum frigida mors anima seduxerit artus.

After *frigida,* which, like all distinct dactyls, we pronounce according to quantity, we *must* make a dead stop on *mors,* and give it its due length and stress; and the cæsura is thus forced upon our notice; but as such hemistichs are rare, the rhythm appears quite strange, and gives more surprise than pleasure. It is indeed so different from that of the many thousand cæsuras of which we shorten the long final, that it may well appear strange; but were we to pronounce *those* according to quantity, the strangeness of *this* would at once disappear; and there are many verses, as we should *then* perceive, which in the first hemistich have the very same rhythm: one, for instance, in the speech from which the line is quoted; another from Dido's preceding speech, "Nusquam tuta fides," "Nec te noster amor:" the only difference between this last and the hemistich in question is, that the choriambus "frigida mors" consists of a dactyl and a monosyllable, whereas noster amor is composed of a trochee and an iambus; a difference which ought not to make any in the rhythm. The cæsura, in its particular part of the verse, should always be felt by the reciter, as quantity ought to be throughout the whole; though neither of them should be regularly marked and weighed upon in recitation: in ours it seldom exists; and on the few occasions where we cannot help admitting it, it seems to disturb the habitual *routine* of our pronunciation, and the sort of unmetrical rhythm we are used to; like a stranger who unexpectedly breaks in upon us, and (whatever may be his good qualities), according to the common phrase, puts us out of our way. That the rhythm of *Et cum frigida mors* appears to us very peculiar, and, as such, to indicate a particular intention in the poet, a curious instance occurred in a correspondence I had with an excellent classical scholar, and a man of a remarkably acute and intelligent mind; he was persuaded that Virgil, by the singularity of the rhythm, meant to express the shudderings felt by Dido, when thinking of the intended suicide: were this a solitary instance of a monosyllable so placed, something perhaps might be said in favour of such a notion; but there are not a few in the ancient poets, and several in Virgil. It would be difficult to discover what expression he could intend by

Sinum lactis et hæc tibi liba Priape quotannis,
Arcades O mea tum quam molliter ossa quiescant,

and others of the same sort. The supposed expression in " Et cum frigida mors," is here produced by the right quantity and the right pronunciation of the cæsura, and is certainly of a harsh character: on the other hand, there are verses, to the first hemistich of which an ample portion of harshness is given by means of the wrong quantity and the total abolition of the cæsura, as in

Frī′gĭdŭs ŏbstīt′ĕrĭt cī′rcŭm praĕcō′rdĭă sā′nguis,

where the choriambus is in our mouths so inarticulately turned over, that if the first *i* were to be changed into *u*, the sound would very aptly indicate the effect of the accentual pronunciation. Some of its steady advocates indeed, if so reproached, might say, like Zanga in the Revenge,

This too is well; the fixed and noble mind
Turns each occurrence to its own advantage:

They might argue, and with truth, that when the blood is chilled, and when the teeth are said to chatter with cold, articulation is impeded; and that therefore the very stammer of ŏbstīt′ĕrĭt, notwithstanding the two false quantities, or rather by means of them, paints the stagnation in the poet's blood much better than the right quantity; there being no difficulty in articulating *obstiterit*. I certainly should not be disposed to admit such a claim to expression, were it likely to be made; but I must allow it is nearly on a par with the other.

The cæsura holds a place in modern languages, as it does in the ancient. In English it is often as strongly marked in our heroics as in the hexameter, and often on finals; as in a line of Pope's, towards the beginning of his Iliad,

> Augur accurst, denouncing mischief still,

the beginning of which answers exactly to Μαντι κακων, as aū′gŭr ācc′ŭrst would be Μἄ′ντῐ κἄ′κῶν, as we are used always to pronounce the iambus, and much better to Μάντι κακ′ων (as if written κακκων), as it is now very much the fashion to pronounce it; but of this new-fangled mode, which, preserving the false quantities, adds a little cacophony, I shall have more to say hereafter. In regard to the number of lines in which there is no distinguishable cæsura, our heroics are more like Homer's than Virgil's: in one respect they differ from both, as from the number of our monosyllables the cæsura frequently ends on one. In Italian I believe they are nearly the same as in English, except in regard to monosyllables, and would be equally injured by laying the accent as in Greek and Latin, " Venuto sei quä′ggĭu," " La bocca sōl′lĕvŏ quel pēc′cătŏr," &c. In French heroic verses of twelve, and in others of ten syllables, the cæsura is essential, and in its most strict

E 2

and regular form its position is never varied; but as it divides every line of twelve syllables into two equal portions, so it divides those of ten into portions that always bear the same relation to one another. From the spondaic character of the French language and poetry, our trochaic pronunciation would mar every thing; as in a line of twelve syllables, which Englishmen repeat with pride,

Le trident de Neptune est le sceptre du monde:

put an accent, as in the English words, on the first syllable of *trident* and *Néptune*, there is neither cæsura nor metre: the same again in a line of ten syllables:

Cette beauté que j'avois incensé.

An Englishman, little acquainted with the language, and not at all with its poetry, would pronounce *cette* as a monosyllable, *beauté*, a trochee, like *beauty*. It appears then, from what has been stated, that in none of the five languages the cæsura should be neglected, and that in some of them it should be carefully observed.

Ease and distinctness of articulation.

Of these qualities numerous examples will necessarily be given in the various quotations: I have been induced however to make a separate article, for the purpose of directing the reader's attention to the manner in which the long syllables are placed in Greek and Latin polysyllables, and to its effect in regard to the qualities just mentioned. Polysyllables in the ancient languages are so happily constructed and divided, the voice resting at such proper intervals on the long syllables, that one might almost suppose it the result of studious attention directed to that particular object; but the general sensibility of the Greeks, from the earliest ages, to euphony of every kind, readily accounts for it, both in their own language, and in the Latin, as derived from it, and formed, though less happily, on the same principles. Among the ancient polysyllables, none is more frequently in use than the choriambus, as cōntĭnŭō; by laying our accent on the second syllable, cŏntīn'ŭŏ, we turn it into an imperfect second peon. The Italians accent the word on the same syllable; but by means of their distinct articulation, and by stopping, and fully dwelling on the vowel, they change the choriambus into a perfect second peon, cŏntī'nŭŏ; and it is thus likewise that they pronounce the adjective and the adverb in their own language. This they have an undoubted right to do, as far as their own language is concerned; for in *that* the rules of ancient prosody and the law of position were not adopted: and though cŏntī'nŭŏ, as a second peon, does not, from the known quantity of the Latin syllables, accord with our classical associations, like *amabile* and *volubile,* yet there is nothing objectionable in the sound or the articulation: in the verb, as *continuàr, continuò,* they lay the accent on the first and last syllables; just as the quantity and cadence of the ancient choriambi requires them to do. Of these

last there are some, to the sound and articulation of
which not even the Italian utterance can reconcile us;
such as cŏnstītĕrĭnt : for as the law of position is not
one of mere convention, but founded in nature, it is
most unnatural to make the first syllable short, when
the vowel is followed by three consonants ; and not
very natural to make the third also short, when followed
by two ; but as *we* hurry over the word, cŏnstīt'ĕrĭnt
is quite abominable. There are some choriambi in
which the case is still stronger ; for with the usual
accent no pronunciation can make them tolerable; as
when in Greek two *cappas* come together ; especially
when in other words they are preceded and followed by
a *chi*, as

Χεύατο κάκκεφ'άλην, χά'ρῐἕν δ' ἤσχῦ'νἕ πρὄσώ'πον.

It is difficult to pronounce the line so accented without
stammering, and without great cacophony ; but when
the accents are on all the long syllables, when the voice
passes on to them, and dwells upon *them* only, the
frequent recurrence of the same sound (for we make no
distinction between the chi and the cappa) is much less
perceived, and the whole is easily articulated :

Χεύατο κάκκ'εφάλή'ν χάρῐέν δ' ἤσχῦ'νἕ πρὄσώ'πον.

Where there is an additional syllable at the beginning,
as in πῆ-λῃιἀδεώ, ĭ-mā'gĭnĭbū's, the same kind of divisions,
the same distinctness of articulation, are preserved ; but
in our recitation there is only one principal division and

resting-place; and in the words πῆλῆϊ̈ᾰδἕω and īmăgīn'ĭ-
bŭs, quantity, euphony, and distinctness, are equally
destroyed. The same principle in the ancient polysyllables, adapting itself to each variation in the circumstances, uniformly prevails, whatever may be the length
of the words; and is as uniformly counteracted by the
rule, wherever the final is long: we therefore are obliged
to say,

ῷ λᾱ'ὅι τ' ἐπῐτἕτρᾱ'φᾰτᾱι,

which, when so accented, must, even from an Italian
mouth, appear comparatively mean and inarticulate:
when rightly accented and divided, as

ῷ' λᾱ'όί τ' ἔπῐτἕτ'ρᾰφᾰτᾱί,

it is neither the one nor the other. In such an ending
of a verse as

νἕφἕλῆ'γἕρἕτᾱ' Ζἕύς

the sound is worthy of the image: in

νἕφἕλῆγἕρ'ἕτᾰ Ζἕύς

most unworthy of both. Words of seven syllables do
not often occur: there is one very beautifully introduced, where Andromache, after her interview with
Hector, sorrowfully retires to her home:

ἄλὄχὄ'ς δἕ φϊλῆ' ὄικὄνδἕ βἕβῆκει
ἐν'τρὄπᾰλῐʹζὄμἕνῆ', θᾰλἕρὄν κᾰτᾰ δᾰκ'ρῠ χἕουσα.

We divide and accent the word, ἔντρὸπ'ἄλἶζὸ'μἔνῇ, always in opposition to prosody, to the flow of the rhythm, and the ease of articulation.

Elisions.

THE general system of versification is obviously the same in the two ancient languages; but there is a difference between our recitation of Greek and of Latin verses, which it is necessary to speak of before I take a view of the various metres, and of the manner each of them is affected by our mode of laying the accent. The Greek language has many intrinsic advantages over the Latin, which were felt and acknowledged by the Romans: the circumstance of the elided syllables being omitted in our editions of the Greek, and not of the Latin poets, is an accidental advantage, relating only to modern pronunciation; but in that respect a very great one, though we do not appear to be at all aware of it. As in the Latin all the elided syllables are left, we have a whole train of supernumeraries, which perpetually clog and retard the movement of the verse; all these as they are printed at length, so we pronounce them; yet as the structure of the verses is the same in both languages, and as in Greek the metre is complete *without* the elided syllables, it evidently follows, that every such syllable in Latin is redundant; it is no less evident, that with redundant syllables, even with one, there can be no metre. To this strange incongruity we are so reconciled by habit, as scarcely to be sensible of it ; but

it will appear in the most glaring light by *restoring* the
elided syllables in a Greek line, as in that language our
habits act in an opposite direction. The instance I
shall give is certainly a very fair one, the elisions being
less numerous than in many I could have produced;
and the false quantities, in our recitation so numerous
and so injurious, that the line seems hardly capable of
farther injury. I shall first put it down as it is printed,
but with the marks of the ictus metricus under the
proper syllables; secondly, with the mark of long on
the syllables we accent, and of short on those we do
not; and thirdly, with the last-mentioned marks on the
same syllables, but with the elided syllables at length.

Τους δ᾽ ελαθ᾽ εισελθων Πριαμος μεγας, αγχι δ᾽ αρα στας.

Τοῦς δ᾽ ἔλαθ᾽ εἶσέλθών Πρῐ́ᾰμός μέ́γᾱς, ἄ́γχῐ δ᾽ ἄ́ρᾰ στᾱς.

Τοῦς δὲ̆ ἐλᾰθε̆ εἶσέλθών Πρῐ́ᾰμός μέ́γας, ἄ́γχῐ δὲ̆ ἄ́ρᾰ στᾱς.

These elided syllables, being here dragged into view for
the first time, have a most strange and barbarous appearance to the eye; and in recitation would no less
shock our ears: yet we may fairly presume, that if
they had been expressed in all our copies of the Greek,
as they are of the Latin poets, we should have pronounced them distinctly, with as little scruple, and as
little sense of ridicule; and consequently have recited
this verse just as I have written it. No one doubts
that the Greeks must always have omitted the elided
syllables both in speaking and writing, and it might
naturally have been expected, that the Romans, who

adopted their metres, their prosody, and their manner of employing elisions, would have done the same; they chose, however, as it appears, to write those syllables at length, though they could not have pronounced them so, without totally subverting all they had adopted. I therefore am led to consider it as merely a *mode* or *fashion* of writing, which did not, and was not meant to, influence the pronunciation; nor is it the only instance of the kind, for we are told by a Latin grammarian, that the Romans sounded the first syllable of *Æneas*, *Æolus*, &c. just as the Greeks did that of Αινειας, Αιολος, although they *wrote* it with what is called an *Æ* diphthong; and he adds, " sic enim *scribimus*," such is our mode of writing. Another instance in a different way may be given, from what was practised in the early times of Roman literature; they then indicated a long vowel by two of the same kind, as *faatum;* and if the double *a* had continued in favour like the *e* diphthong, we should now have in our Virgils, " Italiam faato profugus." " Et si faata deum." How we should have pronounced such words, had they been so printed, may be doubtful; but we certainly should have had the same plea for sounding the additional, that we have for sounding the elided, vowels, their being visible; and the same reason for not making use of such a plea, their being redundant. We do blend the double *a* into one, because only one of them appears: we ought, in the same manner, to blend the elided with the subsequent vowel, *although* both of them appear, and as we say, at least ought to say, keeping the true quantity, " Sic fatus

senior;" so we should also say, "Arm' amens capio."
The principles of versification are so much the same in
Greek and Latin, that there can be little or no difference
in respect to the use and effect of elisions; it may be
right however to give some examples of Latin lines with
and without the elided syllables. The following line
from the Æneid, though it has only two elisions, may
answer the purpose. I shall first put it down as it is
printed, and as we pronounce it; and then shall place
under it a line from the Iliad, with the elisions restored;
when it will be seen that the two first hemistichs, in
which the elisions are, exactly correspond, each having
two redundant syllables, and, by means of them and of
our accents, four trochees in succession:

Primus ibi ante omnes | magna comitante caterva.

Πολλα μαλάόσσάουπω | τις ἐη επεδωκε θυγατρι.

In the second hemistich of the Latin line we have a
fifth and of course unconnected trochee, *magna;* in
consequence of which the two first syllables of *comitante*
are, for want of a preceding long syllable, as māgnā,
likewise unconnected, and left to shift for themselves.
Thus far then there is nothing like metre or rhythm;
at last comes the adonic, which, in Virgil, we generally
pronounce right, " tante caterva:"

Primus | ibi | ante | omnes | magna | comi-tante caterva.

And thus it is that the fiery Laocoon, first and foremost,
" summa decurrit ab arce!"

Elisions in Greek are more numerous than in Latin ; and Homer's verse, from an additional one, hobbles still worse than Virgil's, and, like the other trochees, ἐπι must in some measure be detached, as in the former case, for want of a preceding long syllable, ἐῇ being by our *Latin* rule made a trochee : then comes the adonic, which concludes this curious hexameter :

Πό'λλᾰ | μᾱ'λᾰ | 'ὄ'σσᾰ | οὔ'πῶ | τί'ς 'ἒ'ῇ | ἒ'πὲδῶ'κὲ θῠγᾰ'τρῐ.

When the elided syllables are omitted, and the accents placed on the proper syllables, the metre, rhythm, and cæsura, are restored ; and the first hemistich of the Latin again corresponds with that of the Greek line :

Primus ib' ant' omnes | magna comitante caterva.

Πολλα μαλ' όσσ' ουπω | τις ἐη επεδωκε θυγατρι.

My next example is from Horace's " Ibam forte via," and from the part where he describes his various schemes to avoid the persecutions of the *Garrulus.* I shall begin by putting down the verse (adding part of the preceding and subsequent lines), *without* the elided syllables, and *with* the right quantity, that the reader may see how well the two dactyls at the beginning give the idea of quick motion, and how well the molossus stops it.

misere decedere quærens
Ire mod' ocyus, interdum consister', in aurem
Dicere nescio quid puero.

I will now give it with the redundancies and our accents.

mĭ sĕrĕ dĕcē dĕrĕ quāérĕ ns
I'rĕ mō'dŏ ō'cўŭs, ĭntē'rdŭm cŏnsī'stĕrĕ, ĭn aū'rĕm
Dĭ'cĕrĕ nē'scĭŏ quī'd pū'ĕrŏ.

Instead of the two first dactyls, blended with each other, and thence, with such striking effect, pronounced in a breath, we have three feet, two trochees and the second dactyl *ocyus*, still indeed a dactyl, but no longer with the effect it had when connected and acting in concert with the first; so much depends on the arrangement and interconnection of the feet. Had the elided syllables been omitted, our accent must have been rightly placed on the first as well as on the second dactyl, ĭ'rĕ mŏd' ōcўŭs; but as the case stands, after destroying the united rapidity of the two dactyls, we proceed to destroy the slowness of the molossus, by the usual conversion of it into an amphibrachys, ĭntē'rdŭm; and thus contrive in both places to reverse the expression.

But one single redundant syllable, aided occasionally by our accents, will effectually check the rhythm. The rapidity of Jupiter's command to Iris, βασκ' ἴθι Ἰρι ταχεια', suggests that of the swift-footed goddess when

---

1 We pronounce the first ι in ἴθι and in Ἰρι like the diphthong ιι. It would be much better if in the ancient languages we were always to sound it (as it probably was sounded) like the Italian *i*, our *e*; or at least to do so whenever the vowel is short. Ἐιρι suits the quantity and the metre, but the diphthongal sound of βασκ' ιιθι clogs the pyrrhic, and consequently the opening dactyl.

she obeys it : but if the single elided syllable be restored, as "*βασ'κε ι'θι Ι'ρι*," she is checked at the very
outset, and is any thing but *ταχεια*. In the Æneid the
same sort of command, and nearly the same in the expressions and the rhythm, is given to the other messenger of the gods, the winged Mercury :

> Vad' age nate voca Zephyros :

and it is thus that we deprive him of his *talaria,*

> Vā́dĕ ā́gĕ nā́tĕ vṓcă Zḗphy̆rŏs.

Virgil's line however ends, as his verses generally do, on
an adonic that we pronounce right,

> et—labere pennis :

not so Homer's; in the latter part of it there is a
second elision, and the union of redundancies with false
accents again gives birth to a horrid shapeless monster :

> βᾱσ'κε ῐ'θῐ Ῑ'ρῐ τᾰχειᾰ πᾱ'λῑν τρε͞'πε͞, μη͞'δε͞ ε͞'ᾰ ἀντῆν.

It does, to be sure, crawl most wretchedly,

> " And like a wounded snake, drags its slow length along ;"

but with a length and a slowness (and on such an occasion !) that makes Pope's Alexandrine seem short and
rapid in comparison; the redundancies are required to
complete the Pithon, though in our usual pronunciation
it is no despicable monster. Try all you can to whip

up the trochees, there is no getting them on; there must be a sort of pause after each: the dactyls, when the preceding long syllables are well connected with the pyrrhics, and the ictus metricus duly observed, yet can hardly keep back:

βασκ' ιθι Ιρι ταχεια, παλιν τρεπε, μηδ' εα αντην.

Every thing calls for the omission of the elided syllables in Latin: metre, rhythm, expression, cry out for it. Those, however, who in every way and on all points are attached to the present system of pronouncing, may object, that the suppression of what we are used distinctly to utter would occasion ambiguity: it might just at first, but even then in a very slight degree: no one from the beginning finds any in the Greek; and there can be no reason why, after a short practice, they should find any in the Latin. It may again be objected, that in some instances the expression depends on the distinct utterance of the elided syllable: whenever such instances are produced it will be time to examine them, when I feel very sure that they will not stand the examination. My maxim on the subject altogether is, " Salus metri, suprema lex ;" and all the supposed improvements in the melody of the rhythm, in imitative harmony, and in expression of whatever kind, that are founded on false quantities and false metre, I hold to be universally, what I have shewn them to be in so many instances, mere baseless fabrics.

Hitherto the elisions in both the languages have been

on the same footing; but there is one peculiar to the Latin, that of the *m*, in regard to which there are, in my mind, many difficulties; there would have been none, if nothing farther had been said about it in any ancient author, than merely that it was elided; as then, supposing us to omit the other elided syllables, we should without any scruple omit it likewise: but Quintilian expressly says, that it was not entirely suppressed, but only obscured. His words are, "*Atque eadem illa littera, quoties ultima est, et vocalem verbi sequentis ita contingit ut in eam transire possit, etiam si scribitur*[m], *tamen parum exprimitur, ut* multum ille est, quantum erat, *adeo ut pæne cujusdam novæ literæ sonum reddat: neque enim eximitur, sed obscuratur, et tantum aliquid inter duas vocales velut nota est, ne ipsæ coeant.*" All this was very clear to the Romans of his time, and to their descendants, as long as the Latin remained a living language, and spoken in the same manner; for it only described their constant practice; and supposing there were (as I am led to suspect) some necessary and obvious exceptions to what is here generally stated, they knew where to make them. Quintilian has unluckily given but two examples, both of which, with an

---

[m] These words, "etiam si scribitur parum exprimitur," seem to imply, that the *m* was *generally* omitted in writing; and one might almost be led to infer from them, if the rest of what Quintilian says did not preclude such an inference, that it was generally omitted in speaking; and that when it occasionally appeared to the eye, even then it was but slightly expressed to the ear. At all events the words may lead us to doubt whether the elided syllables were, at all periods of Roman literature, invariably written at full length.

apparent diversity, are in effect of the same kind, for both relate to the elided *m*, when preceded by a long syllable; and it makes a material difference, as we shall see afterwards, when it is preceded by a short one. In each of his examples the *m* may be distinctly, if not harmoniously, articulated, without injuring the quantity, as *mult'm ill' est, quant'm erat;* and that which can be pronounced distinctly may be sounded less so, and therefore more or less obscured. I am here considering the Latim *m*, as having had much the same sound as ours: it has been supposed, however, to have had nearly that of an *n*, but somewhat nasal, as in the French word *faim;* so that the Romans would have made no difference between *circum* and such a word as *circun,* just as the French make none between *faim* and *pain*[n]. What Quintilian says appears to me rather at variance with this supposition: "quid quod pleraque nos illa quasi mugiente littera claudimus *m*, qua nullum Graece verbum cadit." The epithet accords with the sound given to the *m* by the English and the Italians both in their respective languages, and in Latin: and when the Italian *u* is joined to it, and the true quantity observed, there cannot be a more perfect accord between the sound and the sense, than in "mugitusque boum:" *we* give a harsh abrupt utterance to *us* and *um*, passing over the vowel (of which we alter the sound usually given to it in our own language) to the consonants; but the Italians would pronounce the whole as we should if

[n] Dr. Carey, in his instructive work on Latin prosody.

F

written *moogeetoosque booom,* and in such instances the sound prescribed by Quintilian is a great and manifest advantage, which would be lost by any approach to an *n.* The French express the Italian *u* by *ou,* as the Greeks are supposed to have done, but do not, I believe, ever place it before an *m,* and the Latin word *cum* they pronounce as we do, that is, like our *come* and their *comme.* I believe, too, that they never place it before an *n;* and in such words as *chacun, alun,* they totally change the sound of their own *u,* making it a sort of a *e muet,* with a nasal twang. The contrast in Quintilian is between the Latin termination in *m* and the Greek one in *n,* no Greek word, he observes, ending on the former, numbers on the latter[o]: yet if the

---

[o] The following line may, on three points, serve as an example : first, of the frequency of long finals in Greek, all the words ending on a long syllable ; secondly, of our perverse application of the Latin rule, by which we shorten every one of them, in defiance of omegas, etas, and diphthongs :

Α‾ρνων πρωτογονων ρ‾ιξειν κλειτην εκατο‾μβην.

Α‾ρ‾νω̃ν πρω̃το̃'γο̃νω̃ν ρ‾ιξει̃ν κλ‾ει‾την ῖ'κατο‾μ'βη̃ν.

and thirdly, what I had chiefly in view, the frequency of Greek terminations in *ν,* the five words all ending on that letter. Some Greek words, however, in consequence of elision, *do* end on *m,* as " βουλομ' εγω," " κεισομ' ετει," " λισσομ' υπερ," but in these, as the syllable is short, the voice easily may and ought to pass quickly over the final *m,* so as nearly to blend the two words into one ; and in these three instances, into the beautiful foot the choriambus. We on the contrary in all the three instances keep the words quite separate and disjoined : βου̃'λο̃μ' ε‾γω̃, κει̃σο̃μ' ε‾πει̃, λισσο̃μ' υ̃πε̃ρ : all trochees, neither dactyl nor choriambus. When the syllable is long, the voice *must* dwell on it, as " Πατροκλοιο ταφου μνημ' εμμεναι :" more so when there is a stop after the elision, as " και δωμ', εν' ω λιποντες,"

Romans pronounced the *m* as the French pronounce it in *faim*, or the *n* in *pain*, the contrast would be less strong; the consonant would not correspond with the epithet, and in such words as *bo-oom moogentioom* (for so I conceive they must have been pronounced), they would, instead of a very expressive sound, have had one neither expressive, nor harmonious, nor very articulate. Quintilian highly commends the *n* or *ν*, as "quasi tinniens:" now if the Latin *m* had had a sound, which, though nasal and feeble, had still much more of the *n* character than of its own, he might naturally have been led, instead of describing it as *mugiens*, and objecting to it on *that* score, to contrast the dead stifled sound of the false *n*, with the lively, clear, and bell-like tone of the true one. On these grounds I shall go on, supposing the *m* to have had the sound given to it by the English and Italians; though I believe it would make little difference in regard to my positions which of the two might be adopted.

Some consonants readily coalesce with the *m*, as *c* or *x*, *d* or *δ*, *s*, *t*, as in *κμητος, δμωη, Smilax, Tmolus;* we therefore may easily form the same union (as we clearly ought on various accounts) in the following lines, and

---

"*ηβοιμ', ὡς ὁτ' ισ' ωκυροω,*" or where the voice falls suddenly on the final in an iambus, as *τον μεν αγοιμ' ισι νηας.* Such instances, however, though I thought them worth noticing, do not affect the general character of Greek terminations, as they arise, and that very rarely, from an occasional cause, which alters the original termination. The frequency of Latin terminations in *m* is obvious, as in the first line of Lucretius:

Æneadum genetrix, hominum divumque voluptas.

read, "et c'm exustus ager," not "ēt cŭm ĕxūstŭs
āgĕr :" again, "haec d'm agit, ecce," should be uttered
shortly and lightly, like an adonic, not drawled out,
"haēc dŭm āgĭt ēccĕ :" and again, "nec s'm adę'
informis," not "nēc sŭm ādĕŏ ĭnfōrmĭs :" likewise "nec
t'm aversus equos," not "nēc tăm ăvērsŭs ēquŏs."
Others, on the contrary, seem to reject every approach
towards a coalition; as what is called the *j* consonant :
who can articulate "et j'm Argiva phalanx ?" or "jam
j'm efficaci ?" If we make the attempt "vox faucibus
haeret." I believe, however, it is the prevailing opinion
among the learned, that the Romans on all occasions
gave a vowel sound to the *j;* pronouncing Jupiter and
Juno as we should if they were written with a *y, Yupiter*
and *Yuno;* and it is thus that the Italians pronounce
all such Latin words. Without entering for the present upon that question, I shall merely observe on the
one before us, that it is as difficult (I might say as impossible) to articulate "et y'm Argiva," as "et j'm Argiva." The *q* again, as we and the Italians pronounce
it, can as little be articulated under the same circumstances; as, "quanq'm animus." The case is, that the
j and the *q* absolutely require a subsequent vowel,
neither of them being articulate in itself : yet if you
retain the vowel, you must also retain the redundant
syllable. The Romans, however, are said, and I believe
on sufficient authority, to have pronounced the *q* like *c ;*
coquus and *quotidie* like *cocus* and *cotidie;* in which
case that difficulty would be obviated. The *l*, though
it will not coalesce with the *m* at the beginning of a

word, unites with it very pleasingly in other parts, as "castell'm evertere praetor," where the effect is more harmonious than if the *m* were totally omitted. The *r*, likewise, under the same circumstances, may very well be articulated with the *m*, as "mir'm adeo;" but when either of these consonants is immediately preceded by another, I do not conceive how any articulation can take place, as in "templ'm adeo," "tetr'm adeo," and in the well known line,

Monstrum horrendum informe ingens, cui lumen ademptum.

In the first elision, the *m* (and such was Bentley's opinion) must be *totally* omitted ; for no human organs, if I may judge by my own, could articulate "monstr'm horrend':" and though on such occasions an inarticulate stammer might be very expressive, yet in poetry, as in music, mere noise, without rhythm or measure, is not allowable. I should mark the line,

Monstr' horrend'm inform' ingens, cui lumen ademptum,

when the spondees and the length of their finals will be secured by the ictus.

In all these examples, as in those of Quintilian, the elided syllable is preceded by a long one : we must now try the effect of a preceding short one ; and I believe it will be found, that under the most favourable circumstances (as when a *c, d, s,* or *t*, precedes them), the dactyl appears to be clogged ; although, by stopping on the vowel, as in cў-cnŭs or ă-tlās, a dactyl may be formed, as

Induerat; toti-d'm autumno matura tenebat,

Illi me comi-t'm et consanguinitate propinquum;

but with other consonants the dactyl is chained down; as,

Spumantem pater'm et pleno se proluit auro.

It is still more striking where the consonant that precedes the elided syllable is preceded by another: the following hemistich, as we pronounce it,

Corripuere sacram effigiem,

is tolerably articulate prose,

Corripuere sacr' effigiem,

is articulate verse; but pronounce if you can

Corripuere sacr'm effigiem.

There is a line in Horace which is often cited, according to our usual pronunciation, as an instance of extreme harshness, and very justly:

Rān'cĭdŭm ā'prŭm ăntī'quī laŭdā'bănt.

Smoothness, indeed, is as little required for a boar as for a Cyclops; but metre and rhythm, of which there

is not a sign, are always required : they will be found
with harshness enough in

Rancid' a-pr' antiqui laudabant;

but when the *m* in both places is kept, and detached
from the vowel, as

Rancid'm apr'm antiqui laudabant,

the very look of the line is frightful, as the sound
would certainly be, if any organs could be found to
utter it. The rhythm of Horace's hexameters is held
in great and general contempt, and very justly; for it
is our's, not his; when our accents and the ictus are on
the proper syllables, the most uncouth of them, as we
have just seen, have the rhythm which always accom-
panies metre, and is never, in poets of that age, totally
destitute of harmony. In Horace, as might well be
expected from such a writer, it is often highly expressive : we are continually marring the poet's intention by
our false accents, especially when they are aided by
redundancies. I shall give an instance or two, where
the elision now in discussion occurs, that of the *m*.
The following line, from the " Ibam forte," as we pronounce it,

Nĭl hā'bĕŏ quŏd ā'găm, ĕt nō'n sŭm pī'gĕr, ūs'quĕ sē'quăr tē',

is to be sure, with this load of false quantities, and by
means of them and the redundancy, the most drawling
prose : but the character of the *Garrulus* is that of pert,

lively impudence: the line with the right accents and ictus very naturally divides itself into three distinct sentences, well suited to the easy forward style of the speaker.

Nil habeo quod ag', et non sum piger, usque sequar te.

The two first end lightly on dactyls, and in the last the long final of the iambus has an air of determination. The next example has the opposite expression of deliberate slowness: an expression with which we may be said to equivocate: we make and we mar it, for though we shorten and hurry over many long syllables (strikingly so in the opening molossus), yet upon the whole we are over-slow. I shall, for the sake of connection, set down the preceding hemistich, in which we begin the massacre by murdering the adonic.

caŭdāéqŭe pĭ́lŏs ŭt ĕqūínăe
Paŭlā́tĭm vĕ́llŏ, ĕt dḗmŏ ū́nŭm, dḗmŏ ḗtĭăm ū́nŭm.

Without the redundancies, and with the right accents, the whole moves on with a slow deliberate rhythm, that naturally arises from the true metre:

caudaeque pilos ut equinae
Paulatim vell', et dem' unum, dem' eti'm unum.

I shall end this discussion on the *m*, by a very irregular quotation from the "Ibam forte;" the lines, though very near one another, not being in succession, and some of them only half lines: but the *m*, both elided and unelided, frequently occurs in them; and they exhibit perhaps a more striking example than any I have yet given, of the effect of our system, in totally annihilating all that constitutes versification.

Vēn'tŭm ē'răt ăd Vēs'taĕ.
Sĭ' mĕ ā'măs īn'quĭt pāu'lŭm hĭc ā'dĕs, ĭntē'rĕăm sĭ'.
dū'bĭŭs sŭm qū'id fā'cĭăm, ĭ'nqŭit,
Tē'nĕ rĕlīn'quăm ăn rē'm; mĕ sō'dĕs; nŏn fā'cĭăm ĭ'llĕ.
Hĭnc rē'pĕtĭt, mŭltō'rŭm hō'mĭnŭm, ĕt mēn'tĭs bē'nĕ sā'naĕ.

These false quantities, mixed with redundancies, and often occasioned by them, are so flagrant, so crowded together, and they so stare me in the face, that I stare at them again with surprise; and can readily forgive any one who suspects me of having committed some gross error in the marks, as I am almost ready to suspect myself. There is, however, an easy, and I think a very satisfactory, test; it is, that the person who doubts the accuracy of the marks, should carefully follow their guidance in reading the lines; and if he should find, as I am persuaded he will, that they guide him exactly to his usual recitation, he can hardly dispute their accuracy, and must acquit me of having made an unjust charge of such magnitude against all the great scholars throughout these kingdoms. The usual process (with which the reader must by this time be well acquainted, and can apply himself) at once restores metre and rhythm to these lines, and clears them from all their enormities: the only observations I shall make are on the concluding line. In that, the

first elided *m* may be pronounced distinctly without
injury to the metre; "multor'm homin';" but I do not
conceive how an ancient Roman could have so *obscured*
the second, as to be able, with any indication of it, or
of any other consonant, to preserve the quantity, metre,
rhythm, and euphony, in

> Multor'm homin'm et mentis.

I therefore can only suppose that it was entirely
omitted, and that the line must have been pronounced
nearly,

> Hinc repetit; multor'm homin' et mentis bene sanae.

When, if not harmonious, it will at least have metre
and rhythm, and no such intolerable cacophony as
" homin'm et mentis."

Nothing is wanting in the Greek, as far as metre
and rhythm go, but to observe the true quantity, and
the place of the ictus; not so in the Latin, for while
redundancies remain, the true quantity can be of no
use: it would indeed, on many occasions, be worse than
useless, by making us weigh heavily on what is already
an over-load—the long elided syllables; and the slowness
of

> Paulātīm vēllō ēt dēmō ūnūm dēmō ĕtĭām ūnūm,

would go much beyond the Poet's intention. Other
bad effects would occasionally be added to that of slow-

ness : the middle part of the following line, as we accent it,

Nĕc mī'hĭ jăm pā'trĭăm ăntī'quăm spĕs ūl'lă vĭdē'ndi,

does move on, though not with a very free step, or distinct articulation : and although the syllable *am* from its not being elided in *patri'*, is three times repeated, yet, as by our system it is each time made short, we at least pass lightly over it : whereas with the right quantity, but *also* the redundant syllables, the middle part of the verse scarcely moves at all, and the repetition of the termination in *am*, is most unpleasantly pressed on the ear,

Nēc mĭhĭ jām pătrĭām āntĭquām spēs ūllă vĭdēndi P,

with the right quantities, but without the redundancies, the metre is restored, and there is only one rhyme.

Nec mihi jam patri' antiquam spes ulla videndi.

I have now mentioned what I had to offer on the subject of elided syllables, and have stated the difference which occurred to me on that of the elided *m;* a learned

---

P On this solitary occasion, false quantity has certainly an advantage over the true ; I may very well add, " nec habet victoria laudem." The case is, that in our mode, such numbers of long syllables are made short, that the additional length occasioned by the redundancies is balanced ; the one absurdity correcting the other. Charles the Second used to say of a foolish but popular preacher and his audience, " his nonsense suits their's ;" so it is with these absurdities ; they suit each other : it would be a blessing to get rid of them both, but a sin to part them.

friend of mine, who had very much considered the whole of the subject, was for omitting it altogether in recitation : I have given some instances where, in my mind, the euphony would be improved ; and others, where at least no injury in any respect would be done by retaining it : I therefore should wish to follow Quintilian's directions, as far as they can clearly be made out, and practically employed, and no farther ; for he certainly could not intend, that they should lead us to commit false quantities, or to utter inarticulate sounds. Wherever they manifestly produced such effects, it is fair to conclude, that for want of a sufficient number of examples and explanations (unnecessary at the time he wrote), we are not enabled to take a just and full view of the subject. In all cases then, where we cannot give utterance to the *m*, without injuring the metre, or producing extreme cacophony ; or, *a fortiori*, where we cannot utter it at all, in combination with the other consonants, we must do, as my learned friend proposed—omit it altogether.

Elisions in English, French, and Italian.

OF these I shall endeavour to give such an account as may enable the reader to take a general view of the different ways in which elisions have been employed, and to compare them throughout the two ancient and the only modern languages with which I am acquainted. In all that relates to the French and Italian, I shall speak very much under correction ; hoping, however,

that the account will be tolerably exact : in any case
I flatter myself, that by bringing so many elisions, probably for the first time, into comparison, considerable
light will be thrown on the whole of the subject.

English Elisions.

THE elision that most frequently occurs in English
is that of the syllable *ed* in preterperfects and participles; as *disturb'd, retain'd;* its restoration does, in
most instances, the same injury to English, as similar
restorations do to Greek verse : and the grander the
imagery and the diction, the more offensive the injury.
No line is more generally known, or more admired in
those respects, than the opening one of a noble passage
in the *Tempest :*

> The cloud-cap't towers, the gorgeous palaces :

and, in another style of grandeur, the opening of a
simile in the Iliad [q] is familiar to most readers of Homer,
though not the mode of pronouncing it, which I shall
indicate by the marks of the ictus, and that of the
pyrrhic :

> Οἱ δ᾽ ισαν αργαλεων ανεμων αταλαντοι αελλη.

The restoration of the single elided syllable in each,
" the cloud-capped towers," and " οἱ δε ισαν," offends us
almost equally.   There is a line in the Æneid of the

---

[q] Book xiii. 795.

same character with that in the Iliad; and had we been
used to see it written,

> Qualis ub' ad terras abrupto sidere nimbus [r],

we should be shocked at

> Quális ū'bĭ ăd tērr'ăs,

as we now recite, and hear it recited, with great com-
placency.

Dryden, in his ode to St. Cecilia, has introduced a
prodigious variety of metres and verses, from the shortest
to the longest: one of these last, longer than an Alexandrine, he has employed for a noble purpose: he seems
to have thought that the grandeur of the conception
could not be fully expanded in less than seven feet:

> And stamp'd an image of himself, a sovereign of the world.

If you restore the *ed*, such a beginning as " And stamped
an image," taints and vitiates the whole of the verse.
Two of these elisions occur in one of the lines of Milton's beautiful description of twilight:

> Silence was pleas'd: now glow'd the firmament.

By means of the redundant syllable, *pleased* would
become a trochee, and would do—what our converted
trochees are perpetually doing in Latin—would spoil
the cæsura; while the other trochee, *glowed*, would

---

[r] Æn. xii. 451.

spoil the rhythm of the second hemistich; something in the same manner that both of them are spoilt, though we are not conscious of it, in

Heŭ quāé nŭnc tēll'ŭs ĭnquĭt quāe mĕ āéquŏră pōss'ŭnt,

and with an hiatus and a jingle at *quæ me æquora,* the first part jigging on upon trochees, instead of moving slowly on the Virgilian spondee, so appropriate to the expression; especially when the emphatic *heu* and *nunc* are indicated by the place of the ictus:

Heu quae nunc tellus inquit quae m' aequora possunt.

An affecting line in the Orphan contains three of these elisions; the preceding hemistich another:

The poor deceiv'd Monimia
Believ'd, caress'd, and call'd me her Castalio.

What becomes of the pathos (not to mention metre and rhythm), with *deceived, believed, caressed,* and *called?* just what becomes of the metre, rhythm, and sententious dignity, when all the elided *m's* are retained in

Virtutem incolumem odimus;
Sublatam ex oculis quaerimus invidi.

Having given one verse from Dryden's ode, of extraordinary length and grandeur, with a single elision, I shall now put down some short lines from the same ode, of a comparatively light and playful character; the redundancies, though less offensive than in verses of a higher style, are, from the number of them, and their frequent repetition, more ludicrous: the first line is merely to introduce the others:

> The prince, unable to conceal his pain,
>> Gazed on the fair
>> Who caused his care,
> And sighed and looked, sighed and looked,
> Sighed and looked, and sighed again.

Into this sort of namby-pamby rhythm, ill suited even to the lighter part of an ode, we often change, by means of false quantities only, the endings of Homer's hexameters; as

$$μέ'γᾰς ὦδῦ'σᾰτὄ Ζεύς:$$

and, what is of less consequence, some of Horace's; as

$$Născĕ'tŭr rĭdĭ'cŭlŭs mū's.$$

In Greek *any* restoration of an elided syllable does injury to the verse; in English it sometimes does little or none, occasional redundancies at the end being allowed in our versification; but though it may slightly affect the *rhythm*, yet, what can only take place in modern versification, it destroys the *rhyme*. Thus at the end of the line that immediately succeeds those last quoted, we might, considering it singly, and as a blank verse, restore the *ed*; but should be strangely balked (having received a little check at the beginning) when we came to the close of the corresponding line:

At length with love and wine at once oppres-sed,
The vanquish-ed victor sunk upon her breast.

The balk would be a good deal like the well-known one in Scarron :

je crains que vous tombiez,
Vous n' êtes trop bien assuré sur vos jambes.

In Latin we reverse this, and, by pronouncing the elided syllable, instead of destroying, create a rhyme, and certainly where the poet never intended one ; as

Cornua velatarum obvertimus antennarum.
Ad terram misere, aut ignibus aegra dedere.

O'er, as likewise *e'er*, *e'en*, &c. is another of our elisions, and often used both in the simple and in compounds, and, being at the beginning of compounds, must always, if restored, destroy the metre.   In a line of the Paradise Lost,

There the companions of his fall o'erwhelm'd,

we might read *o'erwhelmed;* but neither *overwhelmed* nor *overwhelm'd*.   The simple again, were the *v* restored, would make sad work with one of the many nervous lines in Johnson's masterly imitation of Juvenal :

O'er love, o'er fear, extends his wide domain.

" Over love, over fear" (the rhythm of " over shoes, over boots"), would neither suit the metre nor the subject.   In such words as *'tis*, *'twas*, *'twould*, &c. the vowel at the *beginning* of the word is cut off. I have not observed such an elision in Latin, but in Greek they are not unfrequent; as

Καὶ δὴ 'πὶ κρατι στεφανος, εν πεπλοισι δε.
Παισας καρα 'θωϋξεν· εν δ' ερειπιοις.

We should be shocked at " καὶ δη επι κρατι," or " καρα εθωϋξεν;" and not less were any one to recite the opening line of Dryden's ode:

It was at the royal feast for Persia won:

or from Iago's speech in Othello:

Who steals my purse, steals trash, it is something, nothing,
It was mine, it is his, and may be slave to thousands.

In the examples that have been given, the vowels in *ed* and *it* are totally suppressed, and the consonant in *over;* but the mark of elision in *th'* indicates that the vowel is not to be distinctly pronounced, nor yet entirely suppressed; as in a spirited line of Milton's,

Shook th' arsenal, and fulmin'd over Greece,

we neither say, " shook the arsenal," nor " shook th'arsenal," as if one word; but pass lightly and quickly over the *e* to the *a*, blending the two sounds, as I imagine was frequently done in Greek and Latin elisions. Again in a no less animated line of Shakespear's,

The spirit-stirring drum, th' ear-piercing fife,

the elision is pronounced much in the same manner, easily, and not inharmoniously .

Elisions in French.

THESE very frequently occur; are marked as in the Greek; and, if restored, produce the same effect on metre and rhythm. A few examples will be sufficient; I shall take them from the beginning of the Henriade, restoring the elided syllables:

> Je te implore aujordhui, sévère verité,
> Que la oreille des rois se accoutume à te entendre,
> Ce est à toi de anoncer ce que ils doivent apprendre.

The elided syllables in Latin are, I believe, distinctly pronounced by the French, as they are by us, and, I

ˢ Not so in Warburton's alteration; which, with others of a similar kind, was deservedly brought into notice, and exposed to ridicule, by Edwards, in his Canons of Criticism. Warburton says, " I would read,

> th' fear-spersing fife."

" I suspect," says Edwards, " that this is a false print; it should be, I would *write*; for no man living could *read* such a cluster of consonants." The instance just given one should suppose must stand alone and unrivalled; but there is another of the same *calibre:* all editions but Warburton's have

> " 'tis present death ;"

he assures us that Shakespear wrote,

> " i' th' presence 'tis death :"

" a line," says Edwards, " which seems penned for Cadmus, when in the state of a serpent." These two examples are a match for " Monstr'm horrend'," and " Rancid'm' apr'm antiqui ;" and mark the boundary beyond which elisions cannot be allowed to go.

should suppose, by all the moderns: if so, to such wretched prose as these lines exhibit, Voltaire, in his recitation, must have reduced a large portion of Virgil's hexameters, and of Latin verses in every metre: so must Corneille, Boileau, Racine, and the excellent translator of Virgil, the Abbe de Lille. All these were men, who to a fine ear for harmony, and great acuteness of observation, joined a perfect acquaintance with the best Latin poets, and with the structure of their verses; yet the obvious difference in respect to elided syllables between the Latin and the Greek on one hand, and the Latin and their own language on the other, never appears to have struck them. I must here be allowed to introduce a short anecdote taken from La Harpe: he was at Ferney, and being eager to make some communication to Voltaire, went into his cabinet; but seeing him writing, turned back: " entrez, entrez," lui cria Voltaire, "je ne fais que de la vile prose." He certainly did not mean by this epithet to cast any slur on his own prose, of which he well knew the value; but probably to mark the higher rank and greater difficulty of poetical composition; and perhaps indirectly to give out, that had he been at work on one of his tragedies, *et en verve*, he might not have borne the interruption quite so good-humouredly. The three lines, as I have written them with the redundancies, shew that the vilest of all prose (and scarce worthy of the name, even with the qualification), is verse with the elided syllables at length, and pronounced as written: and this sort of exposition, which, though so very simple and obvious, is not likely to have occurred to him, might have awakened his attention to the effect of pronouncing such syllables in Latin verse; and a number of parallel instances would readily have presented themselves. Thus if "je te implore" destroys the metre, and checks the rhythm, *in limine,* so does with an additional elision, "vēr′tĕ ōm′nĕs tē′tĕ ĭn fā′cĭĕs;" as likewise, "mē′ mĕ ād′sŭm quĭ fē′cĭ ĭn mē′;" and "tē′nĕ ŭt ē′gŏ ăccīp′ĭăr laū′tĕ." The other two French lines are fuller of elisions, but may nearly be matched by two lines, like them in succession, in the Æneid:

Sē′d quĭd ēg′ŏ haĕc aū′tĕm nĕquī′cquăm ĭngrā′tă rĕvōl′vŏ,
Quīd′vĕ mō′rŏr? sĭ ōm′nĕs ūn′ŏ ō′rdĭnĕ hăbē′tĭs Ăchī′vŏs.

In these however, the adonics being pronounced right, the endings go off trippingly; I must therefore add an example or two from Horace, where the adonics are destroyed.

Prī′mŭm năm ĭnquī′răm quī′d sĭt fū′rĕrĕ, hō′c sĭ ē′rĭt ĭn tē′.
dū′bĭŭs sū′m quĭd fā′cĭ′ăm ī′nquĭt
Tē′nĕ rĕlīn′quăm ăn rē′m; mĕ sō′dĕs: nŏn fā′cĭăm ĭl′lĕ.

These beat the French lines, and, so pronounced, must have appeared not less burlesque to an old Roman, than the French lines to a Frenchman; and more is impossible. Had Voltaire's acute mind been led to investigate the subject, he must at once have seen the manifest absurdity of redundant syllables in any language or metre, and the equal absurdity of making,

under any pretext, long syllables short, or short long;
and in the course of an enquiry respecting the pronunciation of the ancient languages, those principal guides
of it, the ictus metricus, arsis and thesis, would hardly
have escaped him. He would probably have taken
them for his guides; and would certainly have found,
that in the verses I have supposed to have occurred to
him, the vile prose he had always been used to make
became verse, the metre exact, the rhythm, even of the
most apparently uncouth among them, no longer displeasing. I will now put them down without the redundancies, and with the right quantities.

Sed quid eg' haec autem nequicqu' ingrata revolvo,
Quidve moror? s' omnes un' ordin' habetis Achivos.
Primum n' inquiram quid sit furer', hoc s' erit in te.

In this last line that most miserably lame conclusion,

qui'd sit fū'rĕrĕ, hŏ'c sĭ ē'rĭt ĭn tē',

runs off in dactyls; just as it would if the words had
been,

quid Lucifer inseret in te.

And how is this striking change effected? simply by
pronouncing the long syllables long, and the short short;
the ictus directing where the stress should be laid, which
it generally does according to the sense and the expression. The line, as we recite it, is a monster; and
it is fair to conclude, that if the elided syllables had
been from the beginning printed at length in Homer,

we should now be reciting Greek as we do Latin hexameters, and with as little sense of ridicule; as, to vary the example,

Αλλα εμε περ προες ωκα, άμα δε αλλον λαον οπασσον.

As the main question now in discussion relates to elisions, quantity is a subordinate consideration; it may be right, however, to mention, that, as far as I have observed, the French pronunciation of Latin differs, in that respect, very materially from ours; as *they* give the full length to a number of long syllables which we make short; and, on the other hand, do *not* give the same rapidity that we do to many short syllables. This difference, however, in the present case, is of little consequence; for as I have before remarked, while the redundancies are kept, the right quantity on long syllables is more injurious than the false; and consequently Voltaire's recitation of the lines I have supposed to have occurred to him, must, so recited, have been more heavy and prosaic than ours. Admitting him therefore to have been convinced of the absurdity of redundancies, of their incompatibility with metre and rhythm, and to have first tried the effect of reciting those verses *without* the redundancies, and afterwards, in his old way, *with* them, he must have been struck with the extreme difference, and might very naturally have exclaimed, during the last operation, "je ne fais que de la vile prose."

Elisions in Italian.

THEY are very numerous, and of various kinds; and, in my view of the subject, might, I think, not improperly be divided into three classes; the first, when they are omitted in writing, as in the Greek; the second, when they are written at length, as in the Latin; the third, where they are, as it were, ready elided without any mark, as *un, amor, poter :* these last have likewise another peculiarity; it is not required, as in the others, that the subsequent word should begin with a vowel. Whether this third class be admitted or not, is of little consequence in regard to my positions: I am inclined to think, however, that the Italians consider it in the same light that I do; for in the Crusca, at the head of the several articles, we have only, *uno, amore,* and *potere;* not *uno, ed un; amore, ed amòr; potere, e potèr;* whereas in other words we find *virtù, virtude, e virtute; bontà, bontade, e bontate;* all equally principals. The second class is by no means a matter of indifference, for it furnishes a strong, I might almost say a decisive, argument for supposing that the Roman mode of writing the elided syllables at length was *merely* a mode; for in Italian, though written at length, they are never distinctly pronounced, but either omitted or blended, so as not to be redundant. A single line will furnish an example of each of the three classes,

Dirò d'Orlando in un medesmo tratto.

The first is the same as

Εγω δ' ες αλλην γαιαν ειμι δη φυγας:

the second like

bellando exhausta sub urbem:

the third *un* is in a great degree peculiar to the Italians[t]. If all the syllables that I have proposed as elided be written and pronounced at length, you have

Dirò | di Or | lando | in u | no me | desmo | tratto,

and fourteen syllables in a hendecasyllable; but without *di* or *uno;* the last syllable of *Orlando,* distinctly and separately sounded, would disturb the metre and the rhythm; *do* therefore is blended with *in;* and may just as readily and pleasantly be blended in the Latin verse with *ex,* as it probably was, and certainly 'not made an extra syllable. In the first and third classes there can be no mistake; in the second, and perhaps the most numerous, foreigners unacquainted with the Italian prosody and pronunciation would naturally do what is done in Latin, pronounce the redundant syllables as distinctly as they are written. In the following line there is only one elision, and of the second class:

Come poiche la luce è dispartita.

Yet by that one the rhythm is checked at the end, with the unavoidable accompaniment of an hiatus, *la luce è;*

[t] *Men' vivo* for *mene,* is on the same footing in Latin.

such as we are perpetually making in Latin, and of the very worst kind, as " Phrygia agmina," " vacua atria ;" extremely offensive even with our narrow *a*, but much more when pronounced by the Italians with their open vowel. I shall go on with the second class of elisions, but with verses containing more of them.

Si va lagnando in questa parte e in quella

is an instance, among many others, of the beautiful manner in which the Italians blend the elided vowels into those of the succeeding words; and of the very opposite effect when all the fourteen syllables are distinctly sounded. But as the mere English reader would lengthen the verse just quoted, so he would be apt to shorten the one I am going to quote :

Che furo al tempo che passaro i Mori :

for though he would add two syllables to the eleven, he probably would give only four feet to the verse altogether, from our strong propensity to the amphibrachys,

Che furo | al tempo | che passaro | i Mori,

when the three terminations in *o* (only one of which is distinctly heard in Italian recitation) would be pressed upon the ear. Terminations on the same vowel, as " che furo al tempo," are often forced into notice by the distinct pronunciation of the redundant syllables, as in one of Catullus's hendecasyllables : I shall mark the quantities as they are regulated by our accent :

Sĕd cīrcŭmsīlĭĕns mōdŏ hūc mōdŏ īllŭc.

What a change when the verse is freed from redundant syllables and a redundant foot, and the cadence is regulated by the ictus!

Sed circumsiliens mod' huc mod' illuc.

The similar terminations are vanished; and what a difference between the false dactyl in the wrong place, "cŭmsīlĭĕns," and the true one, "cumsiliens!" then with what a dead weight do "mōdŏ hūc mōdŏ īllŭc" hang on the ear! Catullus, in this most expressive line, had revived his Lesbia's dead sparrow in all its playful vivacity: by our barbarous pronunciation the poor bird is, like Panthoides, "ter' Orco Demissus." I shall now give some examples of the first and third classes, mixed however, as they so often are, with the second; and shall restore in writing the elided syllables.

> Da rendere molle ogni core rozzo, e scabro,
> E siate certa che il mio onore. mi ha spinto.

We have in Horace, *retaining* the elided syllables, which I have *restored* in Italian,

Ĕt sī'nĕ pŏ'ndĕrĕ ēr'ŭnt, ĕt hŏnō'rĕ īndīg'nă fĕrē'ntur:

and it is evident that *pondere* must no less necessarily, for the metre and rhythm, be a dissyllable and a trochee than *rendere*; and equally evident that *honore* must no less necessarily be an iambus than *onore*. The Italian

dactyl, *rendere,* is made a trochee by eliding or omitting
the final vowel: so are two dactyls in

'Υμεις δε μητερ' ουκετ' ομμασιν φιλοις,

but with this difference, that they could not have been
made such, unless the succeeding word had begun with
a vowel; whereas the Italian dactyl is made a trochee
without any such condition; its last syllable (the law of
position having no more force in Italian than in English) is short before a consonant, as *render molle,* and
rendermi and *renderti,* are dactyls. In Horace's line,
pondere, though a trochee, is written at length as a
dactyl; so are some Italian words under the same circumstances; as

Nel doloroso carcere, ed io scorsi:

and *then* the Italian, like the Greek and Latin words,
must be followed by a vowel. I do not see how an
Italian can think himself justified in destroying Horace's
metre and rhythm by " pōndĕrĕ ērŭnt" and " hŏnōrĕ
ĭndīgnă, with an hiatus each time; and Virgil's, with
more offensive hiatus, in " flūmĭnă āmĕm" and " văcŭă
ātrĭă lūstrăt," when he knows that under the very same
circumstances he would do the very same to Dante and
Ariosto.

In the following line from Tasso,

E quel che'l bello e'l caro accresce all' opre,

the redundancies that are expressed as in Latin are more
than sufficient to destroy the metre and rhythm; yet,

on the other hand, were the redundant vowels to be *totally* sunk in recitation, as

> E quel che'l bell' e'l car' accresc' all' opre,

though the metre and rhythm would be exact, yet the sound and cadence altogether would be more harsh and abrupt than *with* the redundant syllables : and this very strangely points out, that the elided vowels in the ancient languages should, whenever it is possible, be blended, and not entirely omitted. There is a line of Virgil's, in which one of the Italian words, the same in look and sound, occurs; and clearly ought to be blended in the same manner.

> Mĕ bēllŏ ă tāntŏ dĭgrēssŭm ĕt caēdĕ rĕcēntĭ.

Our trochaic pronunciation of dissyllables, added to the redundancy, gives to *bello* and *tanto* the same chiming cadence ; but by blending the elided vowel of the first with *a*, and likewise attending to the right quantity and the place of the ictus, there is no chime, nor even a similarity of cadence ; the other elision should also be blended, preserving the *m* as it is sounded in *smentire*, *smeraldo*,

> Me bell'o a tanto digress'm et caede recenti.

I may observe by the way, that the line, in our mode of pronouncing, is a good instance of the propensity I lately mentioned, as it consists of five amphibrachs. The Italian line with its whole complement of redundancies, open and concealed, has two or three additional feet, and nine or ten additional syllables.

E quel | lo che | il bel | lo e | il ca | ro ac | cresce | alle | opre.

This beats any line I know of in Latin poetry; in Greek there are some that may match it.

'Ως δε ότε αν ανδρα ατη πυκινη λαβη όστε ενι πατρη[x].

What *would* be done to the Greek and Italian poets, were the elided syllables restored, *is* done to the Latin poets, who are most cruelly and unnaturally used by those, who speaking a language so similar and so pre-eminent in all that regards the beauty and harmony of sound and utterance, have the means of reciting Latin poetry, with almost the same perfection as their own.

---

[x] I remember to have seen towards the end of a little thin book, called Farnaby's Rhetoric, a Latin verse composed of a multitude of little words that seemed never to end; but which altogether by dint of elisions formed an hexameter: from its oddness it has remained in my memory, but as I have not seen the book or the verse for above sixty years, I may not put it down quite exactly.

 " Tu in me ita es, hem in te ut ego sum, ac tu me ibi ama, ut te ego amo hic jam."

This strange verse, made for the purpose of shewing how many elisions might be stuffed into one hexameter, may answer a more useful one in this discussion; for when the redundancies are omitted, and the quantity preserved, its rhythm is, without comparison, more harmonious than most of the lines I have quoted *with* their redundancies and our accents. I shall save my readers the trouble of picking out the rhythm, which I shall put down as the words may be connected, and without the endless marks of elision.

 Tin mites hint ut ego, sac tu miba mut tega mic jam.

This may be done merely by applying to the Latin two rules of their own prosody ; the one, never to lay an accent (in the modern sense) on *any* short syllable, but on *all* the long ones: the other, never to pronounce distinctly and at length any elided syllable. I believe that this alone would be sufficient; but the constant observance of the ictus, arsis, and thesis, would be a very useful addition. Redundant syllables are so obviously incompatible with any regular metre, that I cannot help hoping that the time must come, when we shall be as much shocked at " Flūmĭnă āmĕm," and " Vācŭă ātrĭă," as at " Στέμμᾰτᾰ ἔχων," or " Ἔζετὄ ἔπειτᾰ ἄπάνευθε," and the French and Italians equally so; and that we should all as soon think of saying in our respective languages, " Believed, caressed, and called," "Ce est à toi de anoncer," "E quello che il bello e il caro." It would indeed be most strange, if the Latin language were the only one in which elided syllables might be distinctly pronounced without injury to the metre or rhythm ; and we surely must all see and feel the glaring absurdity of having one prosody for Greek, and another for Latin versification ; and must be sensible of the extreme injustice done to the Latin poets, by loading their verses with redundancies, which we omit or blend in those of our own poets; the injury done by them being in all the languages precisely the same.

IN the preceding pages I have endeavoured, and I hope not unsuccessfully, to establish some essential points. First, that what we call *accent* is simply *quantity;* and therefore, when applied to the syllables on which the Romans laid *their* accent or acute, can produce nothing but error and confusion. Secondly, that the ictus metricus, which together with the arsis and thesis was the chief guide of ancient recitation, and should be that of ours, is incompatible with our mode and practice. Thirdly, that it is likewise incompatible with redundant syllables, and therefore cannot be adopted in practice, unless the elided syllables be omitted in Latin as they are in Greek. Fourthly, that as the ictus is the true guide in recitation, so scanning is the true test of metre; and that a verse which, either from its structure, or from the mode in which it is recited, cannot be scanned, is no verse. These are my chief positions. My fundamental maxim, in regard to the pronunciation, no less than the structure of the ancient languages, is, " Salus metri suprema lex esto." Quantity is the essence of metre; metre that of versification; yet it is seldom denied, and in general very openly acknowledged, that both of them, by means of

H

our mode of pronouncing, are in a high degree injured or destroyed. If you urge to the advocates of the system the great and paramount authority of the maxim, and the manifest inconsistency of depriving versification of what is essential to it, their plea is, that the *rhythm* is so much more harmonious, and often so much more expressive, when verses are read by accent, than it would be if they were read strictly by quantity, that the change could not be endured. No position, upon the very face of it, can be more improbable than that which this assertion involves; namely, that the harmony of ancient verses is improved, and in a very high degree, by breaking in recitation all those rules of prosody, according to which they were constructed: the position has however been taken for granted, with little or no examination, and it is high time to submit it to a very strict one, and to try how far it will bear the test. I must begin by observing, that supposing the improvement to be real, and as great as its advocates pretend, it would still be a very inadequate compensation for the destruction of metre; and, among other reasons, because the rhythm, however pleasing it may appear, belongs to nothing, refers to nothing; it is a sort of fanciful cadence, neither prose nor verse, and having little connection with any metrical arrangement; whereas each regular metre has a rhythm intimately connected with its structure, and equally regular, uniform, and consistent; one that can never be altered without altering the structure, which should as inviolably be preserved to the ear as to the eye. My position, which together with the opposite one will be brought to the closest examination, is, that in no case, if considered on fair and impartial grounds, does the accentual system produce any improvement in the rhythm : that in most cases the injury done to it must, on being pointed out, be evident to any candid person; in many without indication, and in some, and those not a few, it is often so strikingly and even ludicrously offensive and absurd, that the blindest advocate for the system must see, and the most obstinate admit, the reality and the extent of the injury. One very material point is here to be considered; whatever improvement in the rhythm, real or imaginary, may be produced by the accentual system, it must obviously be confined to those parts of the verse where the quantity is changed by *means* of the accent, as by its falling on one or more of the short syllables, or on a part only of the long. Wherever in any portion of the verse, or throughout the whole of it, the quantity remains unaltered, to that, and not to accent, the rhythm of such parts, whether more or less harmonious, must exclusively be attributed. This division of property must, in fairness to both, be strictly attended to; so that quantity may have no claim to what is due to accent, nor accent to what is due to quantity. The method I shall constantly pursue, that of placing the accentual mark *over* those syllables upon which we lay the accent, and the mark of the ictus metricus *under* the first syllable of each foot, will shew at one view, and in the clearest manner, the modern and the ancient mode of reciting, and consequently what belongs to

accent and what to quantity. The hexameter, it is well
known, must always begin with a dactyl or a spondee,
the only two legitimate feet, and therefore with a long
syllable: the ictus metricus is invariably on this first
syllable, and consequently the *arsis*, or first elevation of
the hand or foot, from which the regular order of
recitation, as practised by the ancients, proceeds. The
length of this first syllable is of such vital consequence
to the metre and rhythm, that where it is originally and
on other occasions short, it is made long by means of
the ictus, as in Διὰ μεν ασπιδος, Αρες Αρες. On these
accounts, if the first syllable of an hexameter, which is
invariably long in the structure, be short in the recitation, the line is neither of that nor of any other metre,
but a headless monster belonging to none: and I have
thought right to weigh upon this point, as it will soon
be seen that our mode of reciting gives birth to a
numerous brood of these monsters. I shall begin by
considering the four dissyllabic feet, their employment,
and the consequences of their being all reduced to one
by our recitation, to the trochee. It is obvious, that of
the four feet the spondee and the trochee can alone
begin an hexameter: if a spondee, the foot is complete;
and after every complete foot, the next syllable must
invariably be long, so as to form the beginning either of
a dactyl or a spondee: on the other hand, if the verse
begin with a trochee, the foot is incomplete, and the
next syllable must as invariably be short, so that the
trochee may be *legitimatized* by becoming a dactyl; for
otherwise it does not belong to the metre. These two

rules, which are strictly observed in the structure of verses, are everlastingly broken in our recitation, and the same flagrant errors are carried through every part of the verse: and this again I wish the reader to keep in his mind when the various examples are given. When the line begins with a distinct spondee, i. e. of one word, as we always lay our accent on the first syllable, so far accent and ictus coincide, and all is right; but as we lay it on the first *only*, the last being unaccented, becomes short in recitation: and to the ear there is no difference between a trochee made by such a conversion, and a real trochee; none, for instance, between *sēmpēr*, when followed by a consonant, and *sēmpĕr*, when followed by a vowel, as in the well known pentameter,

Et sémper caúsa est cur égo sémper ámem,

or, reversing the order,

Sémper hy'ems semper spirantes frigora Caúri.

Here then, from our mode of pronouncing, is a false quantity, which can never be made without injuring the metre, and, in a great or less degree, the rhythm; in respect to the rhythm, however, this trochaic conversion is as little offensive as any we make; as in

Ἄλλος δ' ἄλλῳ ἐριζε, Ridens dissimulare:

for where the accent and the ictus fall on the same syllables, the rhythm, notwithstanding the false quan-

tity, moves on without any check. Few, I believe, are
aware that they do make one, that they do shorten the
last syllable; and of those who might be made sensible
of it, by being shewn the difference between their pronunciation of the words single, as άλλος, *ridens*, and
when they are joined to an enclitic, αλλός τε, *ridénsque*,
the accent being *then* on λός and *déns*, the greater part
would think the rhythm improved by the trochaic pronunciation, as more rapid than the spondaic. There
can be no doubt, however, from all we have read on the
subject, that an ancient Greek or Roman would instantly have been aware that the syllable and the
rhythm were hurried on, and would have required that
the second syllable, though in a weaker *tone*, should
have the same *length* as the other; and, supposing them
to have heard and reflected on such a pronunciation,
they might very justly have thought, that the rhythm
itself (putting quantity and metre out of the question)
was more pleasingly varied by a long final in the first
word of each line, the second in each having a short
one. When the verse begins with a trochee, which no
farther belongs to the metre than as forming part of a
dactyl, if the subsequent syllable be not short, and
pronounced so, the trochee must remain one. A long
syllable would not be endured in the structure, and
should not in the recitation: in ours the quantity varies
according to circumstances, which ought not to have
any influence: where a monosyllable follows the trochee,
we almost always pronounce it short, as Άσπις αg'
άσπιδ', tristis at ille; and always, I believe, when a

word of more than two syllables, but—an indispensable condition—with a short final, follows the trochee, as φησιν ορεσκωοισιν, ille Tigellius hoc: on the other hand, where such words end on a long syllable, we are very apt to transfer the length of it to the first, and to block up the poor trochee; as, εργον εποιχεσθαι, aere renidescit tellus. The most frequent change of the quantity, however, is in dissyllables; much the greater part of them in Greek, and all in Latin, being accented on the first syllable. The iambus is the only dissyllabic foot that can immediately follow the trochee, and nothing can be better suited to the place; its first short syllable added to the trochee makes *that* a dactyl, and its last long one forms the two words into that beautiful foot the choriambus; as, εργα θεων, sācrǎ cănūnt. But what happens when our accent is laid on the first syllable of each iambus? A metamorphosis takes place, the most strange and unlooked for, especially in the Greek dis-syllable. The epsilon is distinguished by its name and its form, as a short vowel; and in this case it is followed by another vowel, an additional cause of shortness; yet our accent obliges us to weigh upon it, and the poor trochee, that made itself sure of becoming a dactyl by means of the epsilon, finds it converted into an eta, and all farther progress stopped. Such then is the power of accent, in lengthening any vowel upon which it may be laid; and it acts no less powerfully and invariably by its absence than by its presence; for the longest vowel becomes short, simply by being unaccented; and the instance before us is among the most striking. The omega, from its name, its appearance, the authority of poets and grammarians, and in the present case by its being followed by a consonant, might think itself safe from being hurried over like an omicron, yet in spite of these length-giving circumstances, we say ἔργα θέων, and what is only less *strikingly* flagrant, sácra cánunt[a]. Here then, though in so small a compass, the effects of the two modes of reciting are clearly displayed, and distinctly opposed to each other; that our mode, as far as it acts in opposition to the ancient mode, destroys quantity and metre is obvious; is it less so that it equally destroys rhythm? Will the most strenuous advocate for our system venture even to hint, what has so often been boldly asserted, that the improvement in the rhythm compensates the loss of metre? In fact, the injury done to the rhythm is the greatest that could possibly be done in the narrow compass of two dissyllables: as one of the most varied and harmonious beginnings of an hexameter, the choriambus, is changed into two

---

[a] The Romans *did* lay their acute on the first of *cánunt*, which, though no reason whatever for laying our accent on the same syllable, sounds like a reason, and is given as such. But the Greeks did *not* lay an acute on the first of θέων, and they did lay a circumflex, which includes an acute, and does mark length in the strongest manner, on the last. Ask then an advocate for our system, why we lay our acute where the Greeks did *not* lay theirs, and why we omit laying it where they *did* lay theirs? There is, I believe, but one answer, but one reason, that could be given, yet so very absurd a one, that I think he would be ashamed of giving it; namely, that the Romans laid *their* acute on the first of all dissyllables, that we lay ours upon it, and that the Greeks, I presume as a special favour, have been admitted *ad eundem*.

trochees: in point of metre, two successive trochees are inadmissible in any part of an hexameter, and in point of rhythm and cadence they produce the flattest and most absolute monotony. When we lengthen, as in the example just given, a short syllable after a trochee, we *prevent* the formation of a complete foot; on the other hand, when *after* a complete foot we shorten the subsequent long but unaccented syllable, by passing over it to the next accented syllable, as in " αὐτος δ᾽ εξ Ἰ᾽δης," "félix nimírum," the metre and rhythm are injured in a different way. Each of these two hemistichs consists of five long syllables, the uniform cadence of which is diversified by the different places of the ictus, as αυτος δ᾽ εξ Ἰδης, felix nimirum: but our accent being on the first syllable only of the molossus, the first, as usual, becomes a trochee, and the second, a more striking change, an amphibrach, by which three of the five long syllables are shortened, and nothing can be more completely at variance than the structure and recitation. Now it so happens, that a *real* trochee and a *real* amphibrach form an excellent beginning of an hexameter; for they form that of the first line of the Iliad and of the Æneid, Μῆνιν αείδε, Á'rma virúmque. The reader will have observed, that in *all* the four beginnings our accent is on the same syllables, and therefore the cadence must be of the same kind, though that of our *false* trochee and amphibrach, with a shortened εξ and *ix*, may not be thought quite so harmonious as that of the real ones, which, as accent and ictus agree, we pronounce right. The false feet, however, would be very

much in unison with the trochaized iambus at the
cæsura in each line, θεᾰ and cānŏ, as,

Αὐτὸς δ' ἐξ Ἴδης θεᾱ,   Fēlīx nĭmirŭm cānŏ.

As the lines hitherto quoted have begun either with
a distinct spondee or trochee, no example can have been
given of an anomaly upon which I have laid great
stress—that of an hexameter beginning with a short syllable: it is produced very frequently, and in a great
variety of ways, by our mode, and among them by one
that very often occurs: when at the beginning of a
verse, a pyrrhic or a spondee is preceded by a monosyllable, we, according to our constant practice, hurry over
the unaccented monosyllable, in order to dwell on the
accented syllable; as, αλλ' ἴθι, qui cólor; or, with
spondees,

Ενθ' ἄλλοι μεν πάντες επεύφημήσαν Αχαίοι.

Quum vénti posuére omnísque repénte resédit.

In consequence of the practice I have just mentioned
(a very proper and harmless one in our own language,
but most mischievous in those of the ancients), ενθ'
being made short, the hexameter is headless, and the
opening spondee destroyed; and as again, from the
same cause, we hurry over μεν in order to get to the
accented first of πάντες, the second spondee is likewise
destroyed. The rhythm of all the first part till you

come to παντες (accent and ictus being quite at variance)
belongs then exclusively to accent; all from παντες to
the end (accent and ictus agreeing) as exclusively belongs to quantity. This is the first time that their
respective properties have been separated; and I imagine the upholders of the accentual system will not be
much pleased with the idea of such a separation, or
with the portion assigned to them in this or any other
lines I may have occasion to quote for the same purpose. I shall now consider the effect of trochaizing the
dissyllabic feet in the second hemistich. The spondee
is the only one of them that can in *strictness* occupy the
sixth place, the two concluding syllables being equally
long: trochees, however, are frequently put there, the
concluding syllable of the verse being considered as long
from its situation: all such trochees should obviously
be pronounced as spondees; we do the reverse, and
pronounce all spondees in that, as in every other part of
the verse, as if they were trochees. This of course
produces a false quantity, but it is one that, whether at
the beginning or at the end of the verse, but slightly
affects the rhythm; accent and ictus being in both cases
on the first syllable of the spondee.

The dactyl and spondee with which the hexameter is
generally concluded, and which is often called an *adonic*,
forms, in a variety of ways, a most beautiful ending of
a verse; and according as it is well or ill pronounced,
stamps a good or a bad character on the whole of the
line. The rhythm of Horace's hexameters we treat
with the utmost contempt, and with great reason; for

it is our's, not his; and one principal cause of that
contempt is, that his adonics, more perhaps than any
other poet, are often so constructed, that in our recitation
they have neither dactyl nor spondee: we therefore
very naturally conclude that he, who in regard to his
lyrics was called " numerosus Horatius," lost all ear
when he made hexameters. A number of Homer's
adonics are in respect to our recitation as unluckily
constructed; we do not, however, venture to accuse his
ear, but only suppose that on such occasions the good
old bard was dozing: we shall soon know, by means of
the ictus, which are most to blame, the poets or the
reciters. The pyrrhic, as we have seen, may be placed
within one syllable of the beginning of an hexameter,
and we have also seen the effect of trochaizing it. The
iambus may in the same manner be placed within a
syllable of the end of one; and we shall now see the
result of a change in its quantity; and I think must
feel it, if, after pronouncing the two endings I am going
to put down, as we usually do, and as the mark of
accent indicates, we then give to them the ancient
recitation as indicated by the mark of the ictus; αἴκε
πόθι Ζεύς, fórte vírum quém. What is it that in
three short words, and solely by means of one of them,
makes this enormous difference? the difference between
such wretched monotonous prose, as does not deserve
the name even with the qualification, and the genuine
metre and rhythm? It is simply that we pronounce
the two iambi, as the ancients must have pronounced
them in common conversation as well as in poetry, and

as we pronounce our own iambi, such as *abyss* and *below*; and should stare if we heard any one say at the end of a verse, " the dark a'byss be'low :" would a Greek or a Roman have had less cause for staring at πόθι and vírum? The iambus, when so placed in the hexameter, has always, in our mode, the same effect : in Virgil, from whom the present instance is taken, such instances are comparatively rare, though many examples may be found, as " índe lúpi ceú," " íntus áquae vís" " avérsa déae méns." In Homer they often occur, and still more so in Horace, and when so placed, and so pronounced, the iambus is in truth a most mischievous foot, for it at once destroys the dactyl in the fifth, and the spondee in the sixth place. The pyrrhic can only be put within two syllables of the end, where being converted into a trochee it destroys the dactyl in the fifth place, the spondee in the last being seldom affected by it ; as και κύνας ἀργους, quem súper íngens. This conversion again, which makes the verse drop at once and falter in so essential a place, is more frequent in Homer and Horace than in Virgil, from whom however the Latin example is taken. The worst conversion of the spondee towards the end of the verse is where it precedes a molossus, there being a spondee in the fifth place, as πρός τε θνήτων ανθρώπων : verses of that structure, however, are not very frequent, and, in them, a spondee so placed is very rare.

The examples already given shew what injury is done to the rhythm as well as to the metre by the conversion even of a single iambus, spondee, or pyrrhic: the injury as may be supposed spreads wider when two or more of them, especially in succession, occur in the same verse, as, in the same hemistich, " Si quídvis sátis est b," " Et sálsae frúges c," " Sed támen ésto jam pósse haec d." " αλλ' ἀχος· οὐδε μοι ἐστι πάτηρ e." In these, when the ictus is our guide, the cadence of the two dissyllables is diversified in each of the four examples : the hexameter begins with a long syllable, the cæsura rests upon one ; on the other hand, when we are guided by accent, the hexameter is headless, there is no variety in the cadence of the trochaized dissyllables ; the cæsura is spoilt, the long syllable, in spite of it and the ictus, being shortened : by which also the next foot (whether dactyl or spondee) must likewise be destroyed. Some-times on the middle of a verse they spread backwards and forwards, and injure both hemistichs, as

Αλ'λα μοι αίνον ἀχος σέθεν ἐσσεται ὡ Μενελάε.

In the second hemistich the conversion is not a little offensive, when a dactyl, very much required, as coming immediately before a spondee in the fifth place, is destroyed by it, as

'Ο'ς μ' εκελευε Τρώσι σότι στόλιν ἤγησάσθαι.

It is at least as much so when the same two feet come immediately before an adonic that we pronounce right,

---

b Horace, Sat. iii. b. ii. 127.   c Virgil, Æn. ii. 133.   d Lucretius, ii. 906.   e Iliad vi. 134.

for it checks the progress of the rhythm in a very striking manner and degree, the verse appearing at once to falter and break down in that place, as

Ποίκιλον ἀμφ' ωμοίσι σάκος θέτο, βή δε μετ' άλλους.

Instances of this kind are very common, both in the Greek and Latin poets, and the reader will soon learn to observe them; but the conversion is peculiarly injurious where the idea of rapid motion is to be conveyed, and of such lines it may be right to give an example or two: there is one often quoted for its imitative harmony, where Ulysses in the foot-race presses close at the heels of Ajax Oileus.

Ι'χνια τύπτε ποδέσσι πάρος κόνιν ἀμφιχυθῆναι [f].

The dullest reader must feel the difference in every point of view between πάρος κόνιν, and παρος κονιν pronounced nearly as one word. In the same book, a number of similar instances occur, many of them relating to rapid motion of various kinds, as when Diomed, victor in the chariot race, springs to the ground.

Αύτος δ' εκ διφροίο χάμαι θόρε παμφαναοντος.

The active exulting spring of " χαμαι θορε" we destroy; but had the description been that of a wounded and exhausted warrior slowly sinking to the earth, χάμαι θόρε (had there been such words, or could they have been admitted into the metre) would very aptly have suited the expression.

Two successive trochees, as I have already observed, are inadmissible in any part of an hexameter : no more than two in succession have hitherto been produced, and, as I shall now shew, not for want of examples. Three of them often occur at the beginning of a line :

Τῷδε δ' ἐγων αὐτος θωρήξομαι, αὐταρ ὑπέρθεν [g].

In'de tóro páter Aenéas sic órsus ab álto [h].

A'rvo páscat hérum an báccis opuléntet olívae [i].

In these instances, when we are ruled by accent, the three dissyllables have the same vapid monotony that trochees in succession must always have : on the other hand, when we are guided by ictus, they have in three different ways the most pleasingly varied cadence. No other variety can be given to the cadence of the three successive dissyllables ; for three distinct spondees in succession, the verse beginning with one of them (which I believe are not to be found in any poet later than Ennius), have no less monotony than three trochees, and of a heavier kind : they do not however, like the trochees, offend against metre, though like them so grievously against rhythm [k]. I shall now give a few

g Iliad vii. 101.   h Æneid ii. 2.   i Horace, Epist. l. i. ep. 16.
l. 2.

k No variety can be given to the cadence of distinct spondees in succession from the beginning ; for the ictus, as in " sparsis hastis late," must

instances of three successive trochees in the middle of
the verse:

Ἑκτορα-κήρα δ' ἐγω τότε-δεξομαι ὁππότε κεν δη [1].

Tympana-ténta tónent pálmis-et concava circum [m].

And again at the end of it, as

Τευχεα συλησας φερετω-κοίλας ἐπι νῆας [n].

Murmure compressit coelum, sed-éo mágis ácrem [o].

Quod puero cecinit divina-móta ánus úrna [p].

Such endings are not unfrequent in Homer, Lucretius,
and Horace, and sometimes occur in Virgil, as " puppis
tua Tarcho," "ergo age terrae." I will now request the
reader to observe the *division of property* in the lines
that have lately been quoted: he will find that in some
of them, as in Ἀλλα μοι αἰνον-άχος σέθεν-έσσεται ὠ Μενελάε,
as likewise in Ἴχνια τύπτε ποδέσσι-πάρος κόνιν-ἀμφιχυθῆναι,
accent and ictus coincide throughout, except in the converted iambus and pyrrhic; these two therefore, and
these only, belong to accent; all the rest, in fact all
that is harmonious, exclusively to quantity. In others

always be on the same syllable; but if a word of one long or of two short
syllables be put between them, the cadence is varied with the place of the
ictus, as

Sparsis non hastis neque late.

[1] Il. xviii. 115.   [m] Lucret. ii. 618.   [n] Il. vii. 78.   [o] Lucret.
i. 70.   [p] Hor. Sat. ix. i. 30.

I

again, as "I'nde tóro páter Ænéas sic-orsus ab alto," quantity claims no more than the adonic; all the rest is the exclusive property of accent. In Ἑκτορα-κῆρα δ᾽ ἐγω τότε-δεξομαι ὁππότε κεν δη, the middle belongs to accent, the beginning and the end to quantity. In the three lines at the end of the quotations, quantity has a very small share; in the two first of them, only the two dactyls at the beginning, τεύχεα and múrmure; all the rest (even the adonic being destroyed) belongs to accent; to which the whole of the third line from beginning to end exclusively belongs. But indeed the property is so readily and accurately distinguished by the marks of accent and ictus, as they do or do not coincide, that in future I shall on most occasions leave the partition to the reader. The advocates for the accentual rhythm will not be pleased with the portion assigned to them in the verses that have been quoted; but they will above all be displeased at finding that almost all Virgil's adonics, which they had been used to recite so triumphantly at the end of many a hobbling line, as the property of accent, belong solely to quantity, and that only a small part of them, which they had *not* recited with the same exultation, are the property of accent; such as " Junónis éant rés," " avérsa déae méns." Few among them I believe are aware that they make every Latin final and most Greek finals short, and consequently have reduced the four dissyllabic feet to one; and perhaps have not reflected that two trochees in succession are inadmissible in the hexameter: should this be the case, they will have been surprised to find how often, from their mode of recitation, three of them are made to succeed one another in various parts of the verse. What then will any one of them say as I go on increasing the number, the lines growing longer, and the rhythm dragging more and more heavily with each additional trochee? he may well exclaim like Macbeth,

> a fourth! start eyes!
> What! will the line stretch out to the crack of doom?
> Another yet! a seventh! I'll see no more;
> And yet an eighth appears!

All this shall I, like the witches, and with a spice of their malice,

> Shew his eyes, and grieve his heart.

The following line begins with four dissyllables; and the rhythm, with our trochaic pronunciation, has, besides the usual monotony, something peculiarly childish and ludicrous:

> Στάντε πότι πνόιη πάρα θίν' ἅλος, αυταρ επειτα.

The ludicrous effect is not a little owing to the alliteration, of which this is the first example that has yet been given, as others *will* be given.

I shall here observe, that the recurrence of the same letter is offensively pressed on the ear, when the accent is on the first syllable of every word, as πότι πνόιη πάρα, whereas it is but slightly perceived, and without any offence, when the ictus is on the finals of ποτι and πνοιη and when the pyrrhic, παρα, is slightly passed over. I will only add one example of four trochees in the middle of the verse,

Mollia quae-fiunt áer áqua térra-vapores [q]:

and one at the end:

Αἶψᾰ δ' ἔπειθ' 'ἰκᾰνὸν-'ὅ'θῐ Σκᾰίᾱι πῠ'λᾰι ἦ'σᾰν.

I shall now go regularly on increasing the number as long as they last.

5.

Beginning.

Ἔρ'χόμ' ἔχῶν ἔπῐ νῆ'ᾰς ἔπῆν κὲ'κᾰμῶ πόλὲμῐ'ζῶν [r].

Stḗrnĭt ā'grŏs stḗrnĭt sā'tă lāétă bŏūm'quĕ lăbó'rĕs [s].

Middle.

Ὦ̆ φῐ'λῶ̆ι ἦ'τοῐ κλῆ'ρὸς ἔ'μὸ̄ς, χᾱίρὦ δε και ᾱὐτὸ̄ς [t].

Āéŏlĕ nā'mquĕ tῐ'bῐ dῐ'vῠm pā'tĕr ā'tquĕ hŏ'mῐnῠm rḗ'x [u].

End.

Pŏstrḗ'mŏ pḗ'rĕŭnt ῐ'mbrĕs ū'bῐ ḗ'ŏs pā'tĕr āéthĕr [x].

[q] Lucret. i. 145.   [r] Il. i. 168.   [s] Æn. ii. 306.   [t] Il. vii. 191.
[u] Æn. ii. 65.   [x] Lucret. i. 251.

6.

Beginning.

'Ρίμφα θέων ἐπὶ νῆας ἐγὼ δ' ἐπὶ Νέστορα δῖον ^y.

Ϊlle vŏlāt sĭmŭl ārvă fūgă sĭmŭl aēquŏră vērrens ^z.

Middle.

Τίφθ' οὕτως πάρα νῆας ἀνὰ στρατὸν οἷοι ἀλῆτε ^a.

7.

Πρῶτός ἐμῷ ὑπὸ δουρὶ τυπεὶς ἀπὸ θυμὸν ὀλέσσῃς ^b.

Ἢ καὶ ἐμοὶ τάδε πάντα μέλει γύναι ἀλλὰ μαλ' αἰνῶς ^c.

8.

Mālŭĭt ēssĕ dĕūm dĕūs īndĕ ĕgŏ fūrŭm āvĭūmquĕ.

Dēntĕ lŭpŭs cōrnŭ taūrŭs pētĭt ūndĕ nĭsĭ ĭntŭs.

9.

Fĭĕt āpĕr mōdŏ ăvĭs mōdŏ săxŭm ēt cŭm vŏlĕt ārbŏr.

I was bound by my quotation from Macbeth to produce eight successive trochees in a verse: I have been better than my word, for a "ninth appears," but in a Latin verse: I do not indeed recollect having seen more than seven in any Greek line. There is one however in the twentieth book of the Iliad, in which there are at

^y Il. x. 54.   ^z Georg. iii. 201.   ^a Il. x. 141.   ^b Il. xi. 433.
^c Il. vi. 441.

the beginning five in succession, and after a slight interruption three more to the end :

Οἶδα δ' ὅτι σύ μεν ἐσθλος ἐγω δε σέθεν πόλυ χείρων.

So that the hexameter, as we recite it, consists of eight trochees and a monosyllable: the whole of the rhythm belongs to accent: but no one I imagine will be in a hurry to claim the property, any more than that of *fiet áper*, which no less exclusively belongs to it. This last line gains two of its trochees by means of two redundant syllables, *módo* and *sáxum:* now if we pronounced the elided syllables in Greek (as we probably should, were they written, like these in Latin, at length), the Greek verse with seven trochees would gain two more at the end, and, like the Latin one, consist, without any mixture or interruption, of nine in succession :

Η' και ἐμοι τάδε πάντα μέλει γύναι ἀλλα μάλα αίνως:

and we could not, according to our system, pronounce it otherwise.

I have dwelt very fully on the dissyllabic feet, as they are so much employed ; as they give such a connected variety to the rhythm, when each has its appropriate character ; and such monotony and disconnection, when reduced to the trochee alone ; and lastly, because they form a portion of every other foot. I shall next shew the result of our mode on trisyllables, both on the cadence of the word itself, and in regard to its effect, when so changed, on the metre and rhythm. Of the eight trisyllabic feet, two are inadmissible in

the hexameter, the amphimacer, – ◡ –, and the tribrach,
◡ ◡ ◡; I must however be allowed to give some account
of each. The first of them is frequently employed, and
with the best effect, in iambics: but as we accent the
first syllable only, thereby changing it into a dactyl, a
foot not suited to the metre; and as we also change the
iambus, so peculiarly suited to it, into a trochee, to
which the iambus is figuratively said to have an anti-
pathy, the endings of some noble lines in the Antigone
are cruelly injured, and the beginning of one of them
hardly less so :

Ου γαρ τι μοι Ζευς ην ὁ κῆρυ'ξᾱς τάδε,

Ουδ' ἡ ξυνοικος των κάτω θέων Δίκη,

Οἱ τούσδ' εν ἀνθρωποίσιν ὡ'ρϊσᾱν νόμους.

Ούδε σθένειν τοσούτον ὡ'ὀμῆν τα σα

Κηρύγμαθ', ὡς αγράπτα κα'σφᾰλῆ θέων

Νόμιμα δυνάσθαι θνήτον ὀνθ' ὑπέρδραμειν.

The amphimacer is also very much used in sapphics,
every line beginning with one, or with its equivalent.
I will put down one line (though already very much
out of the bounds I had prescribed to myself), in order
to shew the effect of our mode in destroying the metre ;
in reducing its five legitimate to four spurious feet ; in
substituting a sort of sing-song cadence, of which we
are extremely fond, for the genuine and dignified
rhythm ; and in laying the accent and emphasis on an
insignificant monosyllable, instead of one that is truly

emphatic, and essential to the sense and expression : I shall mark the two modes separately :

Me͞rcŭrĭ nãm tĕ dŏ́cĭlĭs măgīstrŏ
Mērcŭrī nãm tē dŏcĭlĭs măgīstrō[b].

I have given an example of the tribrach in the sixth line of the iambics, and have marked it as I think it ought to be pronounced; that is (on the same principle with the pyrrhic, to which it is so closely allied), by passing quickly and lightly over the two first syllables, just touching on the last, and immediately quitting it. The tribrach never appears in its own shape in Greek, though often in Latin hexameters; in these last, as it is written in length, so we also pronounce it, laying an accent on the first syllable, and making it a dactyl, where no real dactyl could be placed; it is always necessarily placed before a word beginning with a vowel, its last is consequently elided and the foot reduced to a pyrrhic, which forms a true dactyl with the preceding long syllable, as

Quam témere in nósmet légem sancímus iníquam.

Sed fúgite O míseri fúgite átque ab lítore fúnem
Rúmpite.

I must just stop to observe how expressively in Virgil's line the ictus drives on the rhythm; and how the false accents, false dactyls, and redundant syllables, seem constántly to be pulling it back.

[b] Horace, b. iii. ode 2.

The bacchius, ᴗ – –, we accent on the middle syllable only, and therefore make the last short, and the foot an amphibrach, as ămāénŏs: this false quantity however, like some others that have been mentioned, and from the same cause, but slightly affect the rhythm; for the first syllable being short, must, in all situations, be the last of a dactyl, and consequently the ictus must be, where the accent is, on the middle syllable, as in

Et properántis áquae per amaénos ámbitus ágros.

Hae látebrae dúlces étiam si crédis amaénae.

The antibacchius, – – ᴗ, we also accent on the middle syllable, and therefore shorten the first : this false quantity sometimes does little injury to the rhythm, as in

Aspíciet partóque íbit regína triúmpho,

the accent and ictus coinciding; but great injury where they do not coincide, as where it begins the verse, the elided syllable being pronounced as usual :

Rĕgi'nă ĕ spē'cŭlís cŭm prī'mŭm ălbē'scĕrĕ lū'cem.

The two dissyllabic feet most changed by our mode, and of which the change is most extensively injurious, are the molossus (– – –) and the anapæst (ᴗ ᴗ –). The molossus, with the same general character, has from the additional long syllable, greater dignity than the spondee. We lay our accent, as in the bacchius and anti-bacchius, on the middle syllable, but with much greater

injury, as we shorten *two* long syllables ; and in making
it, as we do them, an amphibrachys, depart much more
widely from its character : we could not indeed depart
from it more widely, unless we were to turn it into its
opposite, a tribrach. Among the numerous bad consequences resulting from the change, there is one upon
which I have from the beginning laid great stress : it is,
that whenever an hexameter begins, as it so frequently
does, with a molossus, the verse as we recite it is headless[c]. The molossus is highly expressive where ideas of
bulk and force, of sorrow and dejection, of dignity,
with others of a less definite kind, are to be conveyed.
Thus when Nestor, recollecting his victory when but a
stripling, over Ereuthalion, and the size and strength of
his antagonist, says,

$$\text{Τὸν δὴ μῆκιστον καὶ κάρτιστον κτάνον ἄνδρα}^{d}.$$

The continuation of long syllables quite to the pyrrhic
κτάνον, and the marked emphasis on the first and last
syllable of each of the molossi, seem to me admirably
calculated to create and leave a strong impression on
his hearers ; whereas in our mode, the trochees and the

---

[c] There are several verses in Homer, that, according to some grammarians, are, and were meant to be, headless, or, in their language, *ace-
phalous*, such as " Αρις Αρις," " Δια μιν ασπιδος." I am very unwilling to
believe that Homer had such an intention, and am inclined to transfer the
epithet from the verses to the grammarians. The high authority of Hermann
is against any headless verses, and in favour of the otherwise short syllables
being lengthened by the ictus.

[d] Iliad vii. 255.

two jigging amphibrachs (and I speak of the rhythm only) are as much at variance with the expression: and the cacophony of "καὶ καρτίστοῖς" adds to the number of enormities. There is indeed a verse in another of Nestor's speeches, which in point of cacophony and of difficult articulation, two crying sins of our system, goes beyond it:

Καρτίστοι μεν έσαν και καρτίστοις εμαχόντο[e].

No word can have an easy articulation or a pleasing cadence, the pronunciation of which is strongly at variance with the well-founded law of position; and therefore καρτίστοῖ and καρτίστοῖς are unpleasing as single words; but in the middle part of the line, the combination altogether, with the clash of cappas in "ἐσἄν καἴ καρτίστοῖς," can scarcely be uttered by the voice or endured by the ear. In the two lines just quoted, all the four molossi have the ictus on the first and last syllables; and *therefore*, I may add, have the same cadence. But must not the same foot (it may very naturally be asked) have in *all* cases the same cadence, the syllables having the same quantity? Not when the place of the ictus varies: and this apparent anomaly, before I give any other examples of the use and character of the molossus, I must endeavour to explain. I have in a former part slightly touched on the variety that is given to the spondee and to the molossus by means of the ictus: I must now speak more fully on

[e] Iliad i. 367.

the subject, in order to explain what very much requires explanation; namely, the different sound and
cadence that must often be given to them in consequence of the different position of the ictus. In regard
to spondees, which I shall begin with, the first and
second line of the Æneid will furnish very good examples. In the first line there are five dissyllables: two
trochees, two spondees, and an iambus: all these, when
read by accent, are exactly alike; when by quantity,
with a due and constant attention to ictus, four out of
the five dissyllables have a distinctly varied cadence:

> Ar´ma virúmque cáno̱ Trójae qui prímus ab óris.

Trōjaē differs as much from *ōrĭs* as it does from *cănō*:
ōrĭs as much from *Trōjaē* as from *prīmŭs*: for though
the ictus gives to *Trojae* something of the iambic cast,
yet the quantity distinguishes it from *cănō*, as it does
ōrĭs from *prīmŭs*, and on the same obvious grounds.
Cōntrā, vĭrtūs, and all such words, are very naturally
and properly called spondees; but in metre it would, I
think, be better to consider them merely as affording
each of them two long syllables, which, according to
their position in the verse, may form a distinct foot, or
part of two feet; either of two spondees, or of a spondee and a dactyl. When such words begin or end an
hexameter, they *always* form a complete distinct foot;
when in the middle of the line, as it may happen, as

> Contra quid virtus, et quid sapientia possit[f],

> Horace, Sat. i. b. 1.

the first syllable of *virtus* forms the end of a spondee with *quid*, the second the beginning of one (and there-fore has the ictus) with *et*. On the other hand, in

Itáliam fáto prófugus Lavínaque vénit,

we have the spondee *āni fä*, and then the dactyl *tō pröfü; fato* and *venit* having the same difference in cadence as *Trojae* and *oris*. If this manner of consi-dering spondees be proper, it must be still more so to consider the molossus in the same way, as it cannot in any part of an hexameter be a distinct foot. When the verse begins with one, the ictus must necessarily be on the first and the last, and its cadence on that account have some resemblance to the amphimacer; and the same thing takes place when in any part of the verse it comes after a complete foot ; but when after an incom-plete one, *then* the ictus is on the middle syllable only ; and the cadence, with the usual condition of distinction of quantity, has a resemblance to the amphibrachys, as we make its first and last syllable positively short. Here then is another cause, and a very frequent one, of headless hexameters : nor does the mischief stop there, but extends itself to the next foot, as in two successive lines at the beginning of the second book of the Æneid :

Infándum regína júbes renováre dolórem

Trojánas ut ópes et lámentábile régnum,

and accompanied with the usual destruction of the

cæsura in each line. I will next give an example (not a very common one) of two successive molossi in the middle of the same line.

Sólos felíces vivéntes clámat in úrbe.

I hardly need point out, what, when the words are close together, is so obvious; the monotonous chime of *felíces* and *vivéntes,* the precious fruit of false quantities, or the varied rhythm resulting from the true quantity and the ictus. My present object is to shew the reason why two molossi, equally such, must necessarily in the same verse, if the ancient guide of recitation the ictus be followed, have a different cadence. The first of the two molossi succeeds a complete foot, sōlōs, and therefore has the ictus on the first and last: the two first form a spondee, *fēlī:* a long syllable, *ces,* remains, and the next molossus coming after an incomplete foot must have the ictus on the middle syllable; its first forming the *second* syllable of a spondee with the last of the preceding word *cēs vī:* its two last a complete spondee, *vēntēs.* This is the only way in which metre and rhythm can be preserved; for if you place the marks of the ictus on the second molossus as is done in the first, you will find that there will be a redundant syllable, a broken rhythm, and a heavy chime,

Solos felices viventes clamat in urbe.

In order to shew, what indeed is clear enough, that this does not arise from any difference in the two words,

if you transpose them and the marks, the rhythm will
be the same.

Sólos vivéntes felices clámat in úrbe.

An instance occurs in another of his satires where the
same word, a proper name too, must on the same principle have a different cadence at the beginning, and in
the middle of the verse.

Lucíli, qúis tam Lucíli faútor inépte est ᵍ.

We might carry it on still further by means of a verse
made for the purpose, and repeat the same proper name
three times in succession without destroying the metre.

Maecenas, Maecenas, Maecenas, quid Etruscos.

While either Maecénas, Maecénas, Maecénas, or Maecenas, Maecenas, Maecenas, would be equally bad in
the jigging or the drawling way.

I shall now return to a former verse,

Solos felices viventes clamat in urbe,

and to a former position, that the spondee *sōlōs*, and
the two molossi should be considered as furnishing eight

ᵍ Although the iambus, "ἀντιπαθεῖ τῷ τροχαίῳ," yet we often see distinct trochees to the eye in iambic verses which were certainly not meant
to be pronounced as such. They therefore may be considered as furnishing
each of them a long and a short syllable, which the poet arranges so as to
form spondees or iambi.

Ω τεκ·να τεκ·να σφῶν μιν ισ·τι δη πολις.

long feet in succession to the verse, just as if we composed one of eight long monosyllables, which being out
of the jurisdiction of accent (though not always of its
influence) we should read according to quantity,

Sic vos quem non diis jam vult cum clamat in urbe.

So los fe li ces vi ven tes clamat in urbe.

Having made, and I hope satisfactorily, this very
necessary explanation, I return to the use and effect
of the molossus on different subjects and occasions, and
to the injury done to that effect by our mode. The
opening line of a noble simile in the sixteenth book of the
Iliad, offers a very striking contrast between the first
and the last part,

'Ως δ' ὑπο λαιλαπι πασα κελαινη βεζριθε χθων.

In the first the driving storm is hurried on upon
dactyls; when suddenly the rhythm drops on the
spondee, λᾱινῇ, succeeded by the molossus and the
monosyllable, βέβρῖθē χθῶν: and the continuation of six
long syllables to the end of the hexameter, of which
this is a singular instance, and the heaviness of such a
rhythm, especially at the molossus, no less accords
with the torrents of rain that press upon the earth.
In *our* recitation, the dactyl at the beginning is retarded
by the accent on the first of ὑπο, but the great mischief
is in the last part, where after two amphibrachs κἕλᾱινῇ,
and βέβρῖθē, the voice falls on the unconnected monosyllable χθών. It may be supposed that the spondaic

Virgil did not neglect the use of the molossus: the examples are numerous, and he often employs two of them in the same line, as where the loud but awful and mysterious utterance of the Sibyl is described,

> Horréndas cánit ambáges antróque remúgit
> Obscúris véra invólvens[h].

Who, that has any perception of metre, rhythm, or expression, can endure these jigging amphibrachs? the first of the two lines ending with three of them in succession: again where he paints the vast size and terrific appearance of the serpents that attacked Laocoon,

> Horrésco réferens imménsis órbibus ángues
> Incúmbunt pélago[i].

The slowness of the molossus, especially when the three syllables are pronounced in a nearly equal tone, seems peculiarly to accord with an expression of melancholy, but calm resignation; as when Nestor, after recounting his former triumphs in various games, says,

> ἔμε δὲ χρή γήραϊ λυγρῷ
> Πείθεσθαι[k].

Any marked emphasis on any of the syllables would clearly be at variance with the expression; our accent on the middle one destroys it. Another instance in

---

[h] Æneid vi. 99.   [i] Æneid ii. 204.   [k] Iliad xxiii. 644.

some respects of a similar, in others of a different, kind,
occurs in the same book : a book, in which the discrimination of manners, so admirable throughout the poem
on the grandest and the slightest occasions, is, by means
of the games, displayed in a more familiar manner, and
with a singular degree of variety, and even of playful-
ness. The present example is from the part where
Menelaus's resentment against Antilochus, who had
played him rather a jockeying trick in the chariot race,
is appeased by that amiable young man ; who, in the
most candid, respectful, and conciliating manner, ac-
knowledges his fault, and gives up the prize :

Ἡ'ρᾶ, καὶ ἵππον ἄγων μεγαθύμου Νέστορος ὑιος
Ἐν χειρέσσι τίθει Μενελάου· τοῖο δὲ θυμος
Ἰάνθη ¹.

It seems to me, that this molossus, uttered nearly in the
same even tone as the other, no less happily accords
with the expression of that change, which, during
Antilochus's speech, and lastly by his action, was gradually produced on Menelaus; when his heart, which
had been closed against his young friend, was again
opened towards him, and suffused with every feeling
of joy from restored esteem and affection ! Whatever
may be thought of this comment, I am very sure that
with our mode of accenting the word, it is spoilt, in
every point of view, in the place where it stands : there

¹ Iliad xxiii. 594.

is a sort of flippancy in the cadence of the amphibrach, compared with the gravity of the molossus; and here, together with the expression, it as usual destroys the metre and the rhythm. It seems also, in a manner, to affect them in the preceding verse; the voice ought, in some degree, to stop at the end of the spondee which concludes it: yet, as we make that spondee a trochee, and the molossus an amphibrach, it is led to pass on to what we make a short vowel; and τοῖο δὲ θῡμὸς ἰάνθη makes a good ending of an hexameter, though it is impossible to form the beginning of one with Ἰᾰνθῆ. In Virgil's beautiful simile,

> Pŭrpū'rĕŭs vĕ'lŭtĭ cŭm flō's sŭccī'sŭs ărā'tro
> Lănguéscĭt mō'rĭĕns;

nothing can be more truly an echo to the sense than *Languescit*, when the three syllables are pronounced in a slow and nearly equal tone of voice, though somewhat fuller on the first; the voice again gently falling and resting at the cæsura, on the last of *moriens;* nothing can more completely counteract the whole than our amphibrach, *Lānguéscĭt*, followed by one of our spurious dactyls, *mō'rĭĕns*. Again in that affecting image in the Georgics,

> Moerĕn'tĕm ᾰbjūn'gĕns frᾰtēr'nᾰ mōr'tĕ jŭvĕ'ncum [m],

how very different are the rhythm and the expression, when we dwell and seem to linger on the first syllable

[m] Georg. iii. 518.

of the spondee *moērēnt*, and upon that and the last of
ābjūngēns, from what they are when we turn all the
three trisyllables into amphibrachs! *Moĕrēntĕm ăb-
jūngĕns frătērnă:* I must own, however, that the
monotony of our amphibrachs is curiously diversified:
in the first of the quotations from Virgil all the three
were at the end of the line; here they are at the
beginning of it, and most cruelly at variance with the
expression; we shall soon see another diversity, where
their out-of-time jig is no less so. The third line of
the alcaic stanza, a line of great dignity, in the noblest
of all the lyric metres, sometimes consists of three distinct words, an anti-bacchius, a molossus, and a
bacchius; and when each has its appropriate cadence,
nothing can be more happily varied, or better adapted
to subjects of melancholy and dejection, or to those to
grandeur and dignity: of the first there is a striking
example in Horace's ode on Regulus; Īntērqŭe moē-
rēntēs ămīcōs. It is obvious how essential it is to
variety and expression, as well as to metre and rhythm,
that all the long syllables, especially those of the
molossus, should have their due length in recitation:
the reader, if he has attended to the changes that have
taken place, and been pointed out, will readily guess,
that three amphibrachs, which formed either the beginning or the end of two of the hexameters, must form
the whole of the lyric verse, and make it, from a most
expressive one, quite burlesque, " Ĭntērqŭe moĕrēntĕs
ămīcŏs." The burlesque is not less striking in subjects
of dignity, as

Quŏs īntĕr Aŭgūstŭs rĕcūmbĕns;

and in another ode,

famaque et imperi
Pŏrrēctă măjēstăs ăb ōrtŭ
Sōlĭs ăd Hĕspērĭŭm cŭbīlĕ.

The repugnance we feel to give an equal length to the two long syllables of spondees—there being scarcely any, if any, in English—is increased in regard to the three long syllables of molossi, of which foot there are positively none; but, in exchange we have many amphibrachs, as ălīghtĕd, prĕtēndĕr, &c. the foot into which we always convert the molossus. From this circumstance, while the true cadence of the real foot is never heard by us, that of the false one is familiar to our ears: what is still worse, all Greek and Latin proper names, with three long syllables, Ănchīsĕs, Aĕnĕăs, &c. are not less familiar to us as amphibrachs in our own, than in the ancient languages: so also is Aŭgūstŭs, of which the first and second syllables are *always* long, the last frequently. This mode of pronouncing in Greek and Latin—avowedly incorrect—we consider as having the sanction of constant usage, and as having been time out of mind the English mode: but even this sanction (a very feeble one when the errors are evident and flagrant) we cannot claim; for ours is, in fact, a comparatively modern practice: on this subject I may hereafter speak very fully, and on various points of it; at present I shall only touch upon it. Those who are well acquainted with Chaucer, and our old poets of those times, know that most of the dissyllables which we now accent on the first syllable, as *vírtue, hónour,* &c. were then accented, *virtúe, honoúr ;* and in the following line of Chaucer's,

> Saw I Conquést sitting in great honoúr,

were you to accent and pronounce the words as you do in Dryden and Pope, there would be neither metre nor rhythm. It might, I think, be fairly inferred, that they then gave to the Latin words the same accent which they evidently gave to words derived from the Latin, as *virtús, honór,* on the same grounds that we now lay in Latin, as in English, *vírtus, hónor ;* but there is more immediate evidence of their having done so, by means of ancient proper names, which occur in many of their verses : in the two following lines,

> Fairest of fair, O lady mine, Venús,
> Daughter of Jove, and spouse of Vulcanús,

Chaucer, as if in direct opposition to our system and its rules, has accented two finals that are short in Latin, and only occasionally made long by position : he therefore would *perhaps* have accented them in the same manner when they were short in Latin poetry, but *certainly* when they were long.

As Chaucer laid the accent in his own verse on the last syllable of *Vulcanús,* he would naturally do the same when he met with it in a Latin line, and perhaps (for the propensity to lengthen finals was then almost as strong as it now is to shorten them), when it was before a vowel; he therefore would certainly have given the true cadence to the molossus in " Quos inter Augustús recumbens," and no less certainly to those of which the final always is, or may be, long, as *Anchisés*, *Æneás*, or *Amphión*, *Actaeón*.

The anapaest ($\cup \cup -$), as being the dactyl reversed, has been called the anti-dactyl; and such a mixture of resemblance and opposition was well calculated to produce that play in the rhythm, that varied harmony, so desirable in all metrical compositions; and it could scarcely be credited, were the fact less evident, and had we not already seen an instance of the same kind in the iambus, that in our mode of reciting, this abundant source of metrical delight is completely cut off through the whole of the Latin language: for by accenting the anapæst, as we do the dactyl, on the first syllable, we make no difference in quantity or cadence between *Títyre* and *pátulae*.

In Greek there are some exceptions in regard both to the iambus and the anapæst: when in a word of three syllables, as επειτα, the last of them is elided, we preserve the length of what *had* been the middle syllable, and give to επείτ' the true sound of the iambus, but, I believe, in no other case: an instance of each occurs in

Αυταρ επείτ' αυτοισι βέλος εχεπευχες εφιεις [n].

[n] Clarke says that βιλος was pronounced nearly like *belöss*: however that may have been, the final must certainly have been made long: but if in

We follow the same rule in regard to the anapæst; making the last syllable long where there is an elision, short where there is none, as in

Και τους μεν θέραπων απανεύθ εχε φυσιοωντας.

This is very inconsistent and incongruous, as every thing is in our mode of accenting and pronouncing Greek. The *spirit* (if I may so apply the term) of our system is, that we are to lay our accent, or acute, where the ancients laid theirs: this, as I trust has been clearly shewn, is an absurdity founded on the grossest mistake; in Latin however we are at least uniformly and consistently absurd; but even this palliative is lost when we come to the Greek. In the present instance we lay our acute on the first of θέραπων, and make it a dactyl in defiance both of epsilon and omega: is the Greek acute on that syllable? no; it is on the second: and I have no doubt that the modern Greeks, according to their general practice, make the word an amphibrach, θεράπων, which, in regard to quantity, is on a par with our dactyl, and the epsilon, at least, is short. Why then do we not, according to the spirit of our system, lay our accent where the ancient Greeks laid theirs? because our system was exclusively formed on *Latin* accentuation: and our mode of reasoning seems to be this: if θεραπων had been a Latin word, or Latinized like *Sala-*

---

defiance of prosody we choose to make it short, it would really be better to give the same cadence to the two feet and the two hemistichs; and either to say ιπειπ' and βιλος or ιπειπ' and βίλος.

mis, the Romans *would* have acuted it on the ante-
penult; *ergo* we acute it on that syllable, *though* the
Greeks acuted it on the penult. Again why in the
same line do we lay the accent on the final of απανευθ'?
will it be said (for there does not appear to be any
other difference between it and θεραπων, and most other
iambi), because the final of απανευθε is elided? If such
be the reason assigned, on what is it grounded? Certainly not on any practice of ours in Latin; for in that
we never elide *any* syllable: is it that the Greeks laid
their acute on νευθ' when the ε was elided, and not otherwise? Certainly not: for they equally in both cases
laid it on the second syllable, απά. We, therefore, in
this, and in all anapæsts where a final syllable is elided,
have deviated into the true pronunciation, without
having, as far as I see, any sort of reason for so doing;
it would indeed have been a very lucky deviation, if we
had extended it to every other anapæst; as the case
stands, it is merely an incongruity.

To sum up the whole of what I have been advancing,
there is a manifest absurdity in transferring the Latin
mode of accentuation to the Greek; yet we certainly
should not like to follow the Greek mode, and to
say,

Και τους μεν θεράπων απάνευθ' εχε φυσιοωντας:

yet if reading by accent be right, this pronunciation (of
which, as it is contrary to our habits, we feel all the
absurdity both as to metre and rhythm) must be the
true one. All these incongruities and inconsistencies

are at once obviated by observing, what it is so easy
and natural to observe, the rules of prosody, and the
guidance of the ictus: and I shall give a few instances
of the happy effect of doing so in respect to the rhythm,
and to the play and variety of which I have spoken.
The dactyl and the anapæst cannot immediately succeed
each other, like the trochee and the iambus, but must
have at least a monosyllable between them, and then,
as will be seen by the marks of the ictus contrasted
with those of our accent, they play into each other in
the most natural and pleasing manner:

Lḗnĭŏr ac mḗlĭŏr fis áccedénte senécta?

Mārˊmŏrĭs átquĕ ēˊbŏrĭs fábros átque aéris amávit.

In our mode, besides the monotony, there is in the last
of the two lines a chime, by means of the continued
short finals in *mārmŏrĭs ēbŏrĭs aērĭs:* it is very much
softened by the long final, *ĕbŏrīs,* which divides them.
The same sort of arrangement in the higher style of
poetry has an animated effect, when the long final of the
anapæst, fully dwelt upon, falls on the cæsura; a tame
one when it is shortened; as in Helen's reproach to
Paris:

Ηˊλυθες εκ πόλεμου; ὡς ὤφελες αύτοθˊ ολέσθαι:

and in the striking picture of Alecto in the seventh
book of the Æneid:

Réppulit, et géminos eréxit crínibus ángues.

In these two instances, πολέμου and *géminos* are the only words where accent is at variance, but most mischievously, with quantity. Sometimes a second anapæst succeeds the first, as,

> Ἔκτορα δ' ἐκ βελεων ὕπαγε Ζεύς, ἐκ τε κονίης,

where, with our usual contempt and defiance of the visible signs of length we shorten an ω, and an ε long by position. We have again the same arrangement, where Alecto is first brought to our view, and in the most terrific colours:

> tot Erínnys síbilat hy'dris,
> Tántaque se fácies áperit.

The two real anapæsts after the real dactyl, give a varied and energetic rhythm: the two spurious and misplaced dactyls, a rhythm equally tame and monotonous. I may here observe, that two distinct anapæsts in succession are very common; two distinct dactyls do not often come together, especially at the beginning of an hexameter: I only recollect one instance in Virgil, and it rather surprises than pleases:

> Scílicet ómnibus est lábor ímpendéndus et ómnes:

and I much doubt whether, in any poet of a good age, three in succession could be found; whereas there are not a few instances of three successive anapæsts, as,

> Si súbito médium céleri praeciderit ictu°,

° Lucretius, iii. 636.

Me quóties réficit gélidis Digentia rivis:

and there is one instance in the Iliad of four in succession:

Αιθ' ὀφελες ἀγονος τ' ἐμεναι ἀγαμος τ' ἀπολεσθαι.

This difference may be accounted for by what I observed in a former part; namely, that short finals have a tendency to keep words separate and disjoined; long finals to blend and connect them with one another: the instances may serve to exemplify the position. Two successive dactyls are rare; and that they are rare is a proof that they ought to be so: add a third, as *Scilicet omnibus ardua*, and a fourth, *Scilicet omnibus ardua protinus*, and the ear gets more and more tired, as it does with a succession of trochees, and on the same principle, that each word must be a separate unconnected foot, much like the separate unconnected trees and clumps so often dotted about our grounds; while a succession of anapæsts, to go on with the same allusion, are blended, and in a manner grouped, with one another. The attentive reader will have observed, that in the three last quotations the hexameters are headless; and have seen that they must necessarily be so, whenever at the beginning of a verse an anapæst is preceded by a monosyllable. The examples I have given, shew that the analogy and opposition alluded to are productive of many pleasing and striking effects: but there is an analogy and an opposition, of which hitherto no notice has been taken, and that well deserves it. Both

the feet in question are rapid; there is however a difference in the character of their rapidity, and one that
has been very happily marked by Marmontel in a very
few words, " Le dactyl s'élance, et l'anapeste se pré-
cipite." This, I am persuaded, is not, what it may
perhaps appear at first sight, a fanciful distinction, but
one that is founded on the nature of speech : for when
the voice from a long syllable passes rapidly over one or
over two short syllables, as in the trochee or the dactyl,
it seems to spring forwards; and when, on the other
hand, it passes rapidly over one or over two short
syllables to a long one, as in the iambus or the anapæst,
the fall is sudden and abrupt, and well calculated to
impress the idea of what is headlong or precipitate in
motion : the dactylic rhythm, for instance, is suited to
the active and forward spring of a greyhound, the anapæstic to the headlong fall of water. A question may
here be very naturally and properly asked; whether
the distinction has been constantly observed by the best
poets ? By no means constantly, though frequently :
and they may have been perfectly aware and convinced
of the truth of the distinction, and yet have often
thought fit to deviate from it in practice. No one can
doubt that cĭtŭs, răpĭdōs, cĕlér, cĕlĕrēs, are much more
expressive of quick motion than pērnīx, pērnīcēs, vēlōx,
vēlōcēs; yet the poets, as we know, often chose to
employ these last, either for the sake of variety, or from
their being better suited to the verses they were then
constructing ; they therefore, a fortiori, could not have
felt any scruple in employing a dactylic rhythm for the

purpose of expressing rapid motion, though the anapæstic might have been more exactly suited to the
particular kind of it, and vice versa. Two lines of a
simile in the Iliad furnish a very good specimen of the
dactylic rhythm, and its proper application,

'Ως δ' ὅτε κάϱχαϱοδόντε δύω κύνε εἰδότε θήϱης,

Η κέμαδ' ἠε λαγώον επείγετον ἐμμενὲς αἰεὶ.

In these two lines, the rhythm, like the animals, is
always pressing onwards, without any check; for the
only final, δυω, is so joined to κυνε̆, both by the sense
and the rhythm, that when the marks on each are
obeyed, they must be sounded nearly as one word,
δυωκυνε̆, just as in the similar cases already mentioned,
" χαμαι-θοϱε̆," " μαλα-σχεδὸν." In our mode, " 'Ως δ'
ὅτε," " Η κέμαδ'," and above all, " δύω κύνε," act as so
many clogs.

In the second book of the Æneid (line 496) there is
an instance of a mixture of the two rhythms, and where
the expression is almost equally divided: I shall quote
part of what precedes the line in question:

> cum spumeus amnis
> Exiit, oppositasque evicit gurgite moles,
> Fértur in árva fúrens cúmulo.

An almost constant difference between the dactylic and
the anapæstic rhythms strongly evinces their distinct
characters: that marked division and resting-place in

the hexameter, the cæsura, is scarcely perceived, indeed scarcely exists, in the dactylic rhythm; as in that of the two Greek lines; whereas in the Latin line, the long final of a most expressive anapæst towards the end of the verse falls on the cæsura, and with greater effect from being preceded by an iambus, *furens cumulo*.

These instances, the only ones I intend giving at present, are, I think, sufficient to justify Marmontel's distinction, and the principle upon which it is founded. I shall next consider some of the feet of four syllables, and first the choriambus. Of all the various combinations of the four dissyllabic feet, by means of which the sixteen tetrasyllabic are formed, none to my ear and judgment is altogether so happy a one as that of the trochee and the iambus; and it seems to have been a great favourite with the ancients, whether as a single word, or as divided into several.

The place of our accent varies with the different variations; that of the ictus being invariably on the first and the last: when single we accent the second syllable, as *indómitos*, changing it into a second peon, as *inhóspita:* when divided into a distinct trochee and iambus, the *first* of each, as *pérque dómos*, making them both trochees. Where there are three words, the last of them a monosyllable, the accent generally coincides with the ictus, as ἄλλα καὶ ὥς, and the same when there are four monosyllables as ἥ ῥα νυ μόι. We see from these instances, that four syllables in which, as the quantity and the place of the ictus never vary, the cadence ought to be the same, are pronounced in three different ways, and among the numerous examples of inconsistency and incongruity, this is a very striking one; two of three ways must be wrong; and that the last is the right we may be confident from the agreement between the accent and the ictus. We have not many choriambi in English, that is, not many words in which we make the first and last syllable long, and the two middle ones short; and of them none I believe are of Greek or Latin, or perhaps of Saxon origin; several names of towns in Ireland, as Ballynahinch, and of others in the East Indies, as Chandanagore, are true choriambi, though I believe they have not been used in our poetry: *charioteer* is a very poetical word, and often employed by our poets, as

> Chariot and charioteer lay overturned.

We do not indeed, in this last word, give the due length and stress to the first syllable, nor do we sufficiently detach the two middle syllables from each other, so as to give the true cadence; still with those defects this foot has a noble sound, and gives a very pleasing variety to our rhythm, and it would be lucky if we pronounced all the ancient choriambi in the same manner. Unluckily all our words derived from the ancient choriambi, are accented like them on the second syllable, as Elýsian, Arcádian, ambrósial, nectáreous, Castálian, &c. and as these are among the most poetical

---

P Ultramarine and aquamarine are, however, true examples of choriambi of a Latin origin.

epithets in our language, and perpetually made use of by our poets, they tend to confirm us in our pronunciation of the ancient foot. The Italians, who have fewer of such adjectives, accent them in the same manner, as *contínuo, nettáreo*: they however, by means of elided infinitives, as *continuàr, intenerìr*, and of the accented third person of the perfect, as *continuò, intenerì*, have enriched their language with a number of choriambi; what is of more extensive consequence, a a number of long finals (few indeed compared with the number of them in Greek and Latin) have by such means, at its first formation, been given to the Italian; that beautiful language would otherwise have been doomed to the same wretched monotony, to which the *lingua materna* has been so barbarously condemned.

I shall now resume, what I purposely touched upon but shortly, the dactylic and anapæstic rhythms, the last of them being very much connected with the choriambus, and receiving from that foot both variety and energy. The dactylic is most perfect and distinct, when all the finals (the last of course excepted) are short: yet when from the sense and the cadence a long final blends itself with the two short syllables of the subsequent word, the character of the rhythm is but slightly affected, as in the first line of a striking simile in the twenty-second book of the Iliad,

Η῾ʹυτε κίρκος ορέσφιν, ελαφρότατος ϖετεήνων.

The first hemistich is purely dactylic, and when a

strong emphasis, as indicated by the ictus, is laid on
τος in the second, and the two last words are carried on
together in the same forward cadence, the rhythm is
only less purely so. In our mode, not merely the
dactylic, but all rhythm as well as metre is destroyed:
could we indeed overlook these two peccadillos, and
were we to suppose, that after a short flight the hawk's
onward spring was suddenly stopped, ελαφρότατος, from
its very defects, would be no bad imitation of the
wounded bird's irregular vacillating motion as he flut-
tered downwards, though any thing rather than imitative
harmony. The third line of the same simile is an
example of the pure unmixed dactylic rhythm,

'Η' δε τ' υπαίθα φοβείται, ὁ δ' ἐγγυθεν ὀξυ λελήκως.

In this as in most lines where the finals are short,
accent and ictus coincide, and we then give the right
metre and rhythm ; but though we strictly preserve the
quantity, no one I believe ever complained that he
seemed to be scanning the verse, or heard such a
complaint from his audience. I shall take an example
or two of the anapæstic rhythm from the same noble
poem, and also from similes ; the first from a very short
one in the second book ; it is much admired for its
imitative harmony, and with great reason, when the
pronunciation is guided by the ictus, without any, when
accent is our guide,

Αιγίαλῳ μέγαλα βρέμεται, σμαραγει δε τε πόντος.

The wide difference between accent and ictus in this line at once strikes the eye, and it is sufficiently obvious from the marks, that the anapæstic rhythm is changed to a sort of bastard dactyl, γίαλῳ μέγαλα βρέμεται, and that together with the true metre and rhythm, the expression and the imitative harmony are destroyed. There is also another most injurious consequence of our mode of accenting, to which, as strikingly exemplified in the line just quoted, I wish to call the reader's attention. As we think ourselves bound by our system to shorten all long finals in Greek as well as in Latin, we are obliged to lengthen some other syllable in the same word, and frequently, I may say generally, a short one: this not only produces a manifest false quantity, but often transfers the length and stress from an open sonorous vowel or diphthong to a meagre vowel: thus in the line before us, the ictus is on the final ω of αιγιαλῳ, and also at the beginning of the word on the diphthong αι, the accent, and with it the length and stress, on the most meagre of all the vowels, the iota. In the next word μέγαλα, the ictus is on the long open α, the accent on the ε, the very look and name of which indicate shortness and meagreness; and in βρέμεται the stress on the full open diphthong is transferred to the same thin and short vowel. Another very impressive instance of the anapæstic rhythm occurs in a simile, of which the opening line, Ὡς δ' ὑπο λαιλαπι, has already been quoted. I shall put down for the sake of connection, and not for that alone, the three preceding lines;

Τῶν δε τε πάντες μεν πόταμοι πληθούσι ῥεόντες,
Πόλλας δε κλίτυς τοτ' ἀποτμηγούσι χαράδραι,
Ες δ' ἅλα πορφύρεην μέγαλα στεναχούσι ῥεούσαι
Εξ ὁρεων ἐπι κάρ· μίνυθει δε τε ἐργ' ανθρώπων.

The cadence in these four lines is so singularly varied, that I may be excused for dwelling upon it. In the first, the dactyls and spondees are regularly alternate: in the second, the first hemistich consists of spondees only: in the third, the two rhythms are mixed, the middle part anapæstic; the verse has its full complement of dactyls, which impetuously drive on the rhythm quite to the end: in the fourth, and on this occasion, the principal verse, the anapæstic rhythm from the two successive anapæsts (the first of them, ορεων, forming a choriambus with εξ) is most impressive and appropriate; after four successive dactyls, this last line of the simile, as if in correspondence to the first, strikingly ends with a spondee in the fifth place. All this variety, to which even the uniformity of the first line contributes, is injured or destroyed by our mode of accenting, and the consequent change of quantity; by πᾶντές, and πὸτᾶμὸι, in the first, πὸλλᾱς, and κλῑτῡς, in the second, ᾱλᾰ, πὸρφῡρὲῆν, and μὲγᾱλᾰ, in the third, and lastly in the fourth, by ὁρὲῶν, which makes the verse headless, and checks its rapidity; and though we do preserve the length of the cæsura (a rare occurrence), yet the effect of the second anapæst is weakened by the accent on the pyrrhic, ἐπι. The great cause of mischief, however, is the false accent on ὁρεων, for by that, a spurious misplaced dactyl, is substituted for two legitimate dactyls, εξ ορε, and ων επϊ, and the peculiar force and expression of the anapæstic hemistich, arising from the redoubled ictus of the two successive anapæsts, ορεων επι καρ, of course destroyed.

In a former part, when speaking of a trochee at the beginning of an hexameter, I observed that the iambus is the only foot that can succeed it, their union forming the choriambus; on that occasion, I quoted two beginnings of lines, Ε'ργα θέων, and Sácra cánunt; I will here add, that in these two lines a second choriambus, with the usual intervention of one long or two short syllables, succeeds the first,

Ε'ργα θέων-τα ρα-ϖάγχυ μάχης-έπι μήδεα κείρει.

Sácra cánunt-fu-némque mánu-contíngere gaúdent.

This structure seems to have been a very favourite one; and its harmonious and varied cadence, accords either with a quiet, animated, or pathetic expression. In the second book of the Æneid, whence the Latin example is taken, there are many of the same structure; and one, not far from the example, of a tranquil kind:

Témpus érat-quo-príma quiés-mortálibus aégris.

There is one in the second book of the Iliad, which Pope admired for its energy:

Οἱ δ' αρ' ισαν-ὡσ-ει τε πυρι-χθων ϖασα νεμοιτο,

and one in the first book of Lucretius, that presents a most affecting image of Iphigenia :

Múta métu-tér-ram génibus-submíssa petívit.

Horace too has often employed the same structure, and given dignity to one of his hexameters where dignity was required :

Témpla rúunt-an-tíqua deum.

All these choriambi, according to our constant practice, we change into two trochees, by accenting the first syllables of the iambi; and I believe are particularly pleased with the cadence produced by the change. We are indeed quite persuaded that the rhythm of Greek and Latin verses is so much improved by our mode of accenting, as to compensate false quantities and false metre; and this notion, however glaringly observed, is so deeply rooted, that I must endeavour to place its absurdity in every possible light; for that purpose I shall here make use of a test which seems to me perfectly fair and satisfactory, that of substituting for the iambi two spondees, which we pronounce exactly in the same manner, as

Templa rumpunt antiqua divum.

Should we *then* be pleased with the cadence? we well know what an outcry would be made against the substitutes: yet why cry out? the cadence (the only point in question) is not at all altered by the change of the words. The reasons I take to be, first, that we have always acquiesced in *rŭ̄nt* and *dēŭm*, whereas *rūmpŭnt* and *dīvŭm*, though less false in quantity, are new and strange to us; in the next place, we know that the first are metrically right, the second metrically wrong, though we make them both equally wrong to the ear. But can any one, putting metre and prosody out of the question, deliberately prefer the dead monotony of the trochees to the harmonious variety of the choriambi? Such a person may perhaps be found; for, as somebody says, I forget who, or in what play, " when a man is once thoroughly resolved, reason can do no harm:" he must be prepared however to give the same preference to the rhythm of the spondees, or to explain on what grounds he refuses it.

In our language, as I have already observed, the number of *distinct* choriambi, as *charioteér*, is very small, and of those very few are employed in poetry; on the other hand, we have a great number of *compound*, of such as are composed of two, three, or four words, having the cadence which ought to be given to the ancient choriambi of every description: as these are continually made use of by our poets, though seldom noticed with a reference to the foot, it may not be useless to consider their effect in our poetry and versification.

Foster, in his excellent work on Accent and Quantity, speaking of what he calls our common epic verse, and comparing it with the ancient iambic, observes that the latter never admits the trochee, while in the former a trochee placed at the beginning of a verse gives it a peculiar grace and vigour, as

Die of a rose in aromatic pain.

He also observes that Pope has used it oftener than any of our poets; and afterwards says, "in general that nervous springiness and elasticity (if I may so express it), so very observable in his metre, is often owing chiefly to a trochee beginning his line." He then quotes several, marking them not with the accentual, but the ancient marks of long and short, as " grēat ĭn thĕ eārth," " wārms ĭn thĕ sūn," " glōws ĭn thĕ stārs," " līves thrŏugh ăll līfe," &c. I am persuaded his position is right: but I am likewise persuaded, that the effect he speaks of is not merely and solely owing to the trochee at the beginning, but to its being in most instances, as in all that have just been quoted, followed by an iambus, and to their forming by their union a cho-riambus. In the hexameter, a trochee at the beginning of a verse *must* be followed by an iambus: in our heroic it almost always *is:* in the one, two trochees *can* never be in succession; in the other, they *may*, but rarely *are*, and then for the sake of some particular expression, as, according to my way of pronouncing and accenting it, in a line of Pope's which Foster has quoted:

Jūmpĭng high o'er the shrubs ōf thĕ rough ground.

In this instance he has only marked the trochee at the beginning, and, what he considers as one, in the middle, ōf thĕ, leaving the rest to the reader's judgment: but, from his mentioning only two trochees, it seems probable that he read the three first words as a choriambus, " Jūmpĭng hĭgh o'ēr."

This sort of uncertainty with respect both to metre and rhythm could not take place in the ancient languages, where most of the monosyllables have a settled quantity in the language, all of them in the verse; whereas few if any of our monosyllables are positively either long or short, but by varying the accent may be made either the one or the other at the will of the poet or the reader; and in the present case we may say,

Jūmpĭng hĭgh o'ēr thĕ shrŭbs ōf thĕ roŭgh groūnd.

Or,

Jūmpĭng hĭgh o'ĕr thĕ shrūbs ŏf thĕ roūgh groūnd.

In what way Pope meant the verse to be pronounced we can only guess; but as he certainly meant it to be imitative, and not by means of its harmony, I should prefer the rhythm of the lower line; which, very unlike the usual *allure* of his versification, " va par sauts et par bonds," as it ought to do on such an occasion. It is, in my mind, quite necessary for the expression, that a marked accent and emphasis should be laid on *high*, which ensures a second trochee at the beginning; after it there would be two short and a long syllable, forming altogether a choriambus, but which would not give the same impression of a flowing cadence as at the beginning; we should chiefly feel the sudden fall on the long

final, " hīgh o'ĕr thĕ shrūbs." An accent and emphasis
on such words as *of* or *the* could not in any way be
expressive; but by making them both short, the accent
would abruptly, and therefore, on such an occasion,
expressively, fall on the emphatic word *roūgh*; and as
groūnd would also be necessarily long, the verse would
end unusually and strikingly on a spondee, preceded by
a pyrrhic, " ŏf thĕ roūgh groūnd." If my mode of
accenting the verse be thought the right one, or at least
the most suited to the expression, it seems clear that a
trochee at the beginning of an English verse, if followed
by another trochee, though it may give *vigour*, does not
also produce *grace*; if followed by an iambus it produces both. I will now give some examples of choriambi in other English poets: in Shakespear we have
them at the beginning of verse, both in the grave and
playful style, as

> Peáce be to France, if thát France wíll have peáce;

and Prospero's light address to Ariel:

> Cóme with a thoúght.

Sometimes one verse ends and the next begins with a
choriambus, as in Ariel's lively and animated description
of the tempest:

> I boarded the king's ship; nów on the beák;
> Nów in the wáist, the deck, in every cabin,
> I flam'd amazement.

In Beaumont and Fletcher's Rule a Wife and Have a

Wife, I was always struck with the choriambic beginning of Leon's spirited address to the Duke of Medina:

> Nów to my guárd; and if I spare your grace,
> And do not make this place your monument.

In Milton we have various combinations in this foot:

> Vaúnting aloúd, tho' rack'd with deep despair.
> Hígh over-árch'd embower.
> Stóod like a tówer.

And they are found in all our poets, and with the best
effect. In a shorter metre, and a more familiar style, a
verse sometimes consists of two choriambi, as

> Stíll to be neát, stíll to be drést.

Our language indeed seems naturally to run into them in
the most familiar and least elevated of phrases; as *Jáck
in a bóx, Moúse in a cheése, Dót and go óne,* &c. &c.
I heartily wish we could bring ourselves to correct our
accentuation and pronunciation of αϱγάλεων, ἔϱγα θέων,
Indómitos, Sácra cánunt, &c. by *Will o' the Wisp, Búg
in a rúg,* which in their little way have a very perfect
cadence: it would not be of the same consequence if we
took it into our heads to transfer our accentuation of
the noble Greek and Latin choriambi to our little
phrases, yet I should really feel some regret if it
became the fashion to say *Wĭll ŏ' thĕ Wĭsp,* or *Bŭg ĭn
ă rŭg.* I need not avow, what is so clear from the
length and tenor of this article, my fondness for the
choriambus, and my earnest wish that we should on all

occasions give to those in the ancient languages the same quantity and cadence which we do give to them, and with such good effect, in our own : I only hope that many of my readers may feel the same wish and the same partiality.

I shall now consider some of the other tetrasyllabic feet ; and as the reader knows there are fifteen more of them, he may well feel some alarm : I think however I can promise him, that what I shall say of the rest will not amount to much more than what I have been induced to say of this one.

The dispondee, as the name announces, is a foot of great length and gravity : and when a poet wishes some principal image, of whatever kind, whether pleasing, majestic, or mysteriously awful, to be impressed and to remain on the reader's mind, the slowness with which he is to pronounce, and therefore to dwell on the different syllables, is very material.   Thus in the opening line of Virgil's beautiful description of a country life and its happiness, a dispondee is preceded by an interjection :

> O fortunatos nimium sua si bona norint
> Agricolas.

Such is the rhythm of this line when the ictus guides us : how different when we are guided by accent ; and how different the quantity it produces :

> Ŏ fŏrtŭnātŏs nĭmĭŭm sū'ă sĭ bŏnă nō'rĭnt
> Ăgrĭ'cŏlăs.

No spondee, no dactyl (unless we claim as such nĭmĭŭm

and *sūă sĭ*), no cæsura; and the rhythm such as might thence be expected. A line in one of Horace's Satires begins like that of Virgil's; but, what is not common, a second dispondee immediately succeeds the first:

> O fórtunati mércatóres grávis ármis
> Míles áit.

Here the two dispondees are made ditrochees; the line ends with a third, or its equivalent, *grávis ármis;* and the next line begins with a fourth, *Míles áit.* When Homer, in the first book of the Iliad, describes the king of men rising from his seat, the expressive compound epithet is a dispondee:

> Ἡρως Ατρεϊδης ευρυκρειων Αγαμεμνων[q].

We do not only make the epithet a ditrochee, but also the name of the monarch; and if we wished to turn both into ridicule, we could not do it more effectually than by εὔρῠκρεῖων Ᾱγᾰμε̄μνων. In the fourth Georgic, Virgil has employed this foot with great effect, where Orpheus enters the confines of hell:

> Taenárias étiam faúces, álta óstia Dítis
> Et cáligántem nígra formídine lúcum
> Ingréssus.

[q] All such patronymics as Ατρειδης used to be considered as Molossi in Homer as well as in the Latin poets: of late years, I believe, they have been looked upon as choriambi, Ατρειδης. We should equally lay our accent on the second syllable, and make it either Ατρειδης or Ατρειδης. Mr. Knight has divided what has generally been printed as a compound, and writes it ευρυ κρειων, but does not in his notes assign any reason.

Throughout these lines, accent and ictus are almost always at variance : all the three lines are headless, and of the thirteen long syllables in the second line and the beginning of the third, we cut off more than one half, and with them the solemn mysterious character. As far as I have observed, the hexameter seldom begins with a dispondee ; it is generally preceded by a monosyllable, which we always slur over.

The second peon (an iambus and a pyrrhic), as ămābĭlĕ, is a very pleasing combination, and frequently employed in hexameters ; it is one of the few tetrasyllables to which, as having one long accented syllable, we give the right quantity and cadence; it is somewhat remarkable on that account, but more so from our giving, by no means with the same reason, the same quantity and cadence to several more feet of the same general class, and among them to the choriambus. Any change, of whatever kind, in the known established structure of a word, must be wrong: and this change is by no means a lucky one ; for the second peon, though a very pleasing foot, is of a very different character from the choriambus, and therefore very ill suited to the same place in a verse. I must on this occasion employ the *test* which I have already made use of. If then I were to repeat, according to the true quantity, and under the guidance of the ictus, to an advocate for our system,

> Terrificant animos et inania murmura miscent,

my hearer, though unused to so totally different a mode

of pronouncing the first hemistich, and therefore prejudiced against it, could hardly help admitting that the
sound of it filled the ear; that the rhythm went rapidly
on without any check, and was exactly in unison with
that which he himself always gave to the second hemistich : but were I to substitute for the first word a *real*
peon, and begin the verse with *timentibus*, how would
he (unless he happened to feel some suspicion) exclaim
against such a beginning of an hexameter ! yet what
answer could he give, if I asked him to explain in what
consisted the difference, with respect to cadence, between
timéntibus and *terríficant ;* and by what change of pronunciation he could make the last more exactly like the
first, than by the one which he always gave to it. I
might further ask him, whether, if he could not but
allow such a *real* second peon to be a perfectly ludicrous
beginning of an hexameter, he could deny that a *false*
one must at least be equally so. All the ancient distinct choriambi, which have been transferred into our
language, are, as I before observed, second peons, as
nectáreous, ambrósial, &c. they are perfectly suited to
our language and versification : still it is to be regretted,
were it only for the sake of variety, that we have not a
greater number of words, and of poetical words, such as
charioteér, with the ancient choriambic cadence. If
this be a subject of regret in regard to English, what
must it be with respect to Latin and Greek ! the difference between the two cases may be worth noticing.
All such words as *Elýsian, Piérian,* &c. have for some
centuries been used by our best poets with an accented

or long second syllable; their quantity and cadence is therefore established in our language by usage and authority; and we could not, if we wished to do so, restore the quantity and cadence of the original words, without spoiling the metre and rhythm of all verses in which those derived from them have been introduced.

Now the ancient choriambi of every description, substantives or adjectives, proper names of persons or of places, have from the age of Homer preserved the same quantity in the structure of verses down to the present time, as have likewise the Latin choriambi from the earliest times of Latin poetry; in both languages they must have had the cadence which belongs to that quantity; till in an evil hour, and in an age just beginning to emerge from total darkness, *false* quantity, under the name of *accent*, prevailed over the true. Then it was that every distinct choriambus throughout the whole of the Latin had an *accent* (in its new and lengthening sense) laid on the second syllable, and the foot itself, in recitation, completely abolished. The Greeks and Romans seem to have had a just quantity and proportion of different metrical feet, according to their more or less frequent use; they had a number of distinct choriambi and of second peons, and a due number of each: consider then what took place in that age of feeble twilight to which I have just alluded: the distinct choriambi were abolished as such, and by adding them to the already numerous second peons, the number of these last was increased beyond all bounds: the due balance between the two feet, and the pleasing effect arising from their variety and contrast was then destroyed, and a set of spurious feet introduced into places totally unsuited to them, though so perfectly suited to those which had been so absurdly converted. The English reader will be fully sensible of the extent of this absurdity when he sees it applied to his own language: Milton's line,

> Above th' Aonian mount, while I pursue,

we know to be exact both in metre and rhythm; and should with great reason be shocked were any one, in reciting it, to restore the ancient quantity to the choriambus, and still more were he to trochaize, as in the Latin, the two iambi:

> Ābŏve th' Āŏnĭān mount, while I pūrsŭe.

Would Virgil then or his contemporaries have been less shocked, or with less reason, had any one pronounced, as to our shame we do pronounce,

> Āŏnĭŏ rēdĭēns dĕdūxĭ vērtĭcĕ Mūsăs.

The false quantities and false rhythm are nearly on a par in each, but in the Latin instance the verse is headless, as must always be the case when it begins with a distinct choriambus. I have been almost unavoidably led into this renewed discussion on that favourite foot, by means of the second peon. Among the remaining feet, some are often, some seldom, used in hexameters; others in scarcely any metres: none of them seem to

M

require any particular notice; but one circumstance, respecting them and the whole catalogue of feet altogether, must not be passed over. I have already shewn, that by laying our accent wherever the Romans laid their's, and no where else, we have left them but one dissyllabic foot in their language, and not more than two trisyllabic; we have gone on much in the same manner with the tetrasyllabic, to which, as to the others, grammarians have given distinct names, accurately stating their respective quantities; and of these last the different combinations. The manner in which we convert and reduce them, so strikingly displays the power of accent, in lengthening short, and shortening long syllables, and the mischievous effect of that power when ill applied, that I am inclined to place the whole before the reader in one general view, and I imagine in a point of view that is not likely to have been thought of: I shall put at the head of each class, or of each division of it, a foot which we pronounce right, our accent being on its *only* long syllable, when it will be found that a certain regular number of the other feet seem to give up the quantity and cadence belonging to them, and to adopt those which belong to their leader; so that they lose their identity and distinct character, though they retain their names. In drawing out this sort of scheme, I shall place the accentual mark over the syllable upon which we lay the accent, and the marks of long and short over *all* the syllables, to shew the quantity, whether right or wrong, that is produced by the accent. I shall put the *real* quantity of each foot immediately after its name: by such means I hope the scheme will have as much clearness as such different marks will allow of.

DISSYLLABIC.

Trochee (– ◡) ā′rmă; iambus (◡ –) ā′măns; spondee (– –) ā′rmănt; pyrrhic (◡ ◡) ā′măt.

TRISYLLABIC.

First division, under the dactyl.

Dactyl (– ◡ ◡) tēgmĭnĕ; anapæst (◡ ◡ –) rē′cŭbăns; amphimacer (– ◡ –) ī′ndĭgĕns; tribrach (◡ ◡ ◡) cē′lĕrĕ.

Second division, under the amphibrachys.

Amphibrachys (◡ – ◡) rĕdū′ctă; bacchius (◡ – –) hŏ-nē′stăs; antibacchius (– – ◡) ăstū′tă; molossus (– – –) rĕstrī′ngĕns.

TETRASYLLABIC.

First division, under the ditrochee.

Ditrochee (– ◡ – ◡) că′ntĭlē′nă; dispondee (– – – –) fō′rtŭnā′tŏs; second epitrite (– ◡ – –) pē′rmănē′bănt; fourth epitrite (– – – ◡) ā′dvĕntā′rĕ.

Third peon (◡ ◡ – ◡) ălĭē′nŭs; antispast (◡ – – ◡) rĕcŭsā′rĕ; ionicus a minore (◡ ◡ – –) Dĭŏmē′dĕs; first epitrite (◡ – – –) să′cĕrdō′tĕs.

Second division, under second peon.

Second peon (◡ – ◡ ◡) ĕgē′ntĭă; proceleusmatic (◡ ◡ ◡ ◡)

hŏmĭ′nĭbŭs; choriambus (– ◡ ◡ –) ĭndō′mĭtŏs; first peon
(– ◡ ◡ ◡) ĭngrē′dĕrĕ; dijambus (◡ – ◡ –) ămāénĭtăs;
fourth peon (◡ ◡ ◡ –) cĕlē′rĭtăs; third epitrite (– – ◡ –)
dĭscō′rdĭaĕ; ionicus a majore (– – ◡ ◡) fŏrtĭ′ssĭmŭs.

There is an odd sort of regularity in most part of
this scheme: the leaders of the first and of the second
division of trisyllables have each four followers; the
leaders of the first and second division of the tetrasyllables each of them eight: this however is only a singular
coincidence: the truly surprising part of it, and most
strikingly to my purpose, is, that out of twenty-eight
ancient feet, twenty-two have disappeared in our recitation! and by means of such lengthening of short and
shortening of long syllables as would have made an
ancient lift up his hands and eyes. What if some
capricious modern despot, such as Nero or Caligula of
old, were to issue out an order, that all the harps and
other many-stringed instruments throughout his domi-
nions should be so tuned as not to have more than one
fifth part of the original notes! should we then expect
the poor dismayed musicians to execute all they had
been used to perform with the same full and varied
harmony, the same effect and expression, as when the
strings were tuned in the old method? he would then
do what that capricious despot Modern Accent has done
in respect to versification: we however are not to be
pitied like the distressed musicians, being persuaded
that with our six feet alone, but under the guidance of
accent, we give more harmony and expression than

could possibly be done under that of quantity, with the whole ancient complement of feet. And now having given this ample specimen of our dexterity in regard to feet and syllables, I must give some of equal dexterity in lengthening and shortening entire verses; and they are such as may well surprise those who have not, as I have, paid great attention to the subject. We all readily acknowledge that the hexameter, as its name indicates, consists of six feet, neither more nor less; will it then be believed, even when the examples are brought forward, that in our recitation some hexameters in Latin, many in Greek, have only four feet; a very large number only five; about the same number, I should guess, have six; no inconsiderable number advance to seven; several to eight; and one or two as far as *nine!* If, indeed, diversity in the number of feet were the main object in versification, our mode of reciting and altering Greek and Latin verses would be perfection; for we proceed upwards from the lowest of four feet in a sort of chromatic scale, by half feet between all the whole ones, up to nine, the ne plus ultra of lengthening. I must admit however that I am obliged to use the word *feet* with great latitude; and should it be contended that many of those I call by that name have little if any pretensions to it, I must own the fact to be so. It seems to me, however, that those who read by the rule of accent, and are therefore free from that of quantity, have very naturally, wherever the two are at variance, feet of their own, and a prosody of their own, solemque suum sua sidera norunt, though not of a very bright and luminous kind: perhaps however, what, for want of another term, I call *feet*, might be termed *divisions:* I shall mark them as such, and cannot see how the verses can be divided in any other manner; or, in fact, any other feet than those within the divisions. I shall begin with a line already quoted.

Four feet.

'Η'ρως | Ατρείδης | εύρυχρείων | Α'γαμέμνων.

Or, lest Mr. Knight's separation of ευρυ and χρειων should be objected,

Σμερδάλεον | δ' ἐβοήσεν | ἐποτρύνων | Ο'δυσήα.

There are much fewer of such lines in Virgil than in Homer, and generally in the Latin poets; there is one however in the second Georgic of a very striking rhythm and expression, but most cruelly injured in other respects, besides that of being curtailed by our accents, as the reader will fully perceive by the marks, especially when compared with these of the ictus:

Sā'xă pĕr | ĕt scō'pŭlŏs | ĕt dĕprē'ssăs | cŏnvā'llĕs.

Four feet and a half.

Σῦμπᾶ'ντᾶς | τοῦς δ' οὔτῖ | δῦνή'σεᾱῖ | ἄχνῦ'μἕνὄς | πἕ'ρ.

Five feet.

As to instances of these, " circumstant undique," the opening line of Virgil's first Eclogue has no more:

Tī́ty̆rĕ | tŭ pā́tŭlaĕ | rḗcŭbăns | sŭb tḗgmĭnĕ | fā́gi,

and the four succeeding lines are equally pentameters, though all of a very mongrel kind; such likewise are the first seven lines of the first Georgic.

Five and a half.

Nĕc sṓlĕăs | fḗcĭt | sū́tŏr | tā́mĕn | ĕst sā́pĭĕns | Qūó.

Six feet.

The following line, which comes next to the seven pentameters in the Georgics, may serve as a specimen, a favourable one indeed, of our hexameters, and of the feet which compose a part of them;

Lǐ́bĕr | ĕt ā́lmă | Cḗrĕs | vḗstrŏ | sǐ mū́nĕrĕ | tḗllus.

Six and a half.

Sǐc ā́nǐmǐs | jū́vĕnŭm | fū́rŏr | ā́ddǐtŭs. | Ī́ndĕ | lū́pǐ | cḗú.

Seven.

Ĕxclū́sŭs | qŭi dǐ́stăt | ā́gǐt | ū́bǐ | sḗcŭm | ḗăt | ăn nṓn.

Seven and a half.

Σῶ́μᾰ δὲ | ὀίκᾰδ᾽ | ἔμὸν | δὄ́μὔενᾰι | πᾰ́λῐν | ὄ́φρᾰ | πῠ́ρὸς | μὲ᾽.

Eight.

Οἶδᾰ | δ᾽ ὅ́τι | σῠ́ μὲν | ἴ́σθλὸς | ἔ́γὼ | δὲ σὲ́θὲν | πὅ́λῠ | χὲ́ίρων.

I shall add another verse of eight feet, as it comes almost immediately after the five pentameters at the beginning of Virgil's first Eclogue,

Nă̄mquĕ | ĕ́rĭt | ĭ́llĕ | mĭ́hĭ | sĕ̄mpĕr | dĕ̄ŭs | ĭ́llĭŭs | ā́ram.

Eight and a half.

Ḗrgŏ | ū́bĭ | mĕ̄ ĭn | mṓntĕs | ĕ́t ĭn | ā́rcĕm | ĕx | ū́rbĕ | rĕmṓvi.

Nine.

Fĭ̄ĕt | ā́pĕr | mṓdŏ | ắvĭs | mṓdŏ | sā̄xŭm | ĕ́t cŭm | vṓlĕt | ā́rbor.

A series of hexameters beginning with a verse of four feet, and proceeding regularly by half feet to nine, is so ludicrously and beyond all measure preposterous, that if the statement cannot be proved false and groundless, the system must be given up, as having produced such a monster of absurdity and incongruity. The incongruity, though quite apparent from the accentual marks only, is more strikingly so, when they and their results are compared with those of the ictus. While we act under that ancient guide, the hexameter has always its exact number of feet, and, what is very material, of legitimate feet; the verse cannot be pressed downwards below, or raised upwards above the right number. Again, to take it in another point of view, those verses to which in our usual recitation we give the right quantity and rhythm, such as Αὖτις ἔπειτα, are easily divided into six portions, each containing a legitimate dactyl or spondee : and such verses could not be depressed or raised below or above the standard. In such verses too there are some striking circumstances and coincidences; no final (that at the end goes for nothing) is long; no word in them has more than one long syllable, on those *only* we lay our accent, and therefore neither lay it on any short syllable, nor leave any long one unaccented. From this it happens that our accentual mark is always on the same syllables with the ancient mark of long, and that the ancient mark of short is on all the unaccented syllables; on these occasions too, our accent, like the ictus, is on the first syllable of each foot, and the marks coincide; the whole coincidence may be thus indicated,

Αὖτῐ́ς ἒ | πεῐτᾰ πὲ | δὄ́νδε̆ κῠ | λῐ́νδε̆τὄ | λᾱ̆́ᾰς ἂν | αἴδης.

" These," it may be said, and with some contempt, " are neither more nor less than the common scanning divisions:" exactly so: and as the ancients did not disdain to make use of such a test, why should we? try it on the lines I have quoted, and see whether any of them, from four to nine feet, even those of six feet, such as they are, will stand it; none of them will: yet by placing our accent on *all* the long syllables of any one among them, and on none of the short, the same scanning divisions with all the coinciding marks may at once be made, as

Sáxa per | ét scopu | lós ét | déprés | sás cón | válles,

or, omitting of course the redundant syllables,

Fíet a | pér mod' a | vís modo | sáx'm ét | cúm volet | árbor.

This is the *test;* but in *recitation* you quit it with its
six uniform divisions, and make such as are suggested
by the rhythm, sense, and expression, as

Saxa per et scopulos | et depressas convalles.

Fiet aper | mod' avis | modo sax'm | et cum volet | arbor.

All this is extremely useful to my purpose in itself, and
likewise as a preparation for a statement which I have
reason to think is of a convincing kind, for it struck
some of my learned friends to whom I shewed it, and
among them Dr. Parr, in that light. My chief object
in these pages has been to shew what has so strongly
been denied, that when in our recitation accent is at
variance with quantity, the rhythm is more or less
injured, never improved. I have shewn in various
instances, the efficacy of that ancient guide, the ictus,
in directing us steadily to the genuine rhythm : I now
hope to enforce all that I have advanced, by means of
a suite of hexameters, gradually differing from one
another. In the first of them, as in an example or two
already given, there is a general and exact coincidence
between accent, quantity, and ictus: in the second,
accent is throughout on the same syllable with ictus,
but not on *all* the long syllables : in the third, accent
(as in the second) coincides with ictus, but is on one
short syllable : in the fourth, accent is in one instance
only on a different syllable from ictus : in the fifth, in

two instances: and so they go on with an additional
instance in each succeeding line, till the last exhibits
an exact converse of the first, accent and ictus being
completely at variance throughout the whole of the
verse. I shall mark the true place of the ictus in every
verse, but shall put an asterisk under the mark when
the accent is on a different syllable, and on that syllable
shall put the accentual mark.

Αὖτῑς ἔπειτᾰ πεδόνδε κύλῐνδετο λᾶᾰς ἀναίδης.

Ἦ', καὶ κῡ'ᾰνέῃ'σῐν ἔπ' ὄφρῦσῐ νεῦσε Κρονῑων.

A'rcădĕs ō' mēᾰ tū'm quăm mō'llĭtĕr ō'ssă quĭē'scant.

Οἰωνοῖσῐ τε πᾶ'σῐ, Διὸς δ' ἐ'τελεῖετὸ βουλη.

Quādrŭpĕdā'ntĕ pū'trĕm sōnĭtū quā'tĭt ū'ngŭlă cā'mpum.

Rā'dĭt ĭ'tĕr lĭ'quĭdŭm cē'lĕrĕs nĕ'quĕ cō'mmŏvĕt ā'las.

Hĭ'ŏnĕς βο'ŏωσῐν ἐ'ρευγο'μενῆς 'ᾰ'λος ἔ'ξω.

Sĭ pĕ'tĕrĕt pĕr a'mĭcĭ'tĭ'ĭm pā'trĭs ā'tquĕ sŭ'ăm nĭ'l.

Ὣς φᾱ'τὸ, τὸν δ' οὔτῐ προ'σεφη νε'φελῆγε'ρετᾰ Ζεύς.

The reader, who has already been prepared by many
occasional examples, will, I hope, feel entire conviction
from this regular suite of them in regard to what I have
throughout been endeavouring to impress on his mind.
He will at once perceive, that as long as we steadily

follow the ictus and its guidance, the rhythm goes on without any material check, though we should not strictly observe the quantity; but that where we neglect, even in a single instance, to follow the guidance of the ictus, there, and in that place, the verse immediately begins to falter; the falterings are uniformly increased with each additional instance in each successive verse, till in the last, where the deviation is as complete as the coincidence was in the first, every vestige of metre and rhythm totally disappears. I shall now make a remark or two on some of the lines. In the second, there being no accent on και, we are apt to pass over it too quickly, but the rhythm is scarcely affected by it, and the fault is as slight a one as can well be made. In the third line, the accent, according to our rule, must be on the first of *méa;* and if weighed upon, as it is on many other occasions, both metre and rhythm would be injured: I believe however that in this and similar instances the rule is very much softened in practice, and that we lay a stress on the *e,* and pass rather quickly over *mea* to the strongly accented monosyllabic *tum* at the cæsura, and that we do *not* pass quickly over *quam,* though unaccented; these however, though they accord with rhythm and expression, are, in respect to our system, deviations which on some occasions we feel to be expedient for the sake of the expression; on others we give full length and stress to the short syllable, as in the very next line:

Vestra méos olim si fistula dicat amores :

and in

> Si méa cum vestris voluissent vota Pelasgi.

Fourth line. The reader must be aware from former examples how extensively the false accent on the word Δῖὸς injures the metre and the rhythm, the dactylic flow of which is instantly checked by it ; one dactyl preceding it, πᾱσῐ Δῐ, is destroyed by our lengthening Δῐ, and another after it, ὄς δ' ἔτὲ, by our shortening ὄς, so that the trochee, πᾱσῐ, and the pyrrhic, ἔτὲ, are both left in the lurch. The fifth begins triumphantly with accent and ictus on the same syllables, but the triumph is short ; dánte is stopped by pū'trĕm, but after a check or two ends happily on an adonic. Sixth : no dactyl, spondee, or any rhythm, till you come to the adonic. Seventh : no dactyl, spondee, metre, or rhythm, from first to last : it ends on two trochees. Eighth : ditto, and even worse : one polysyllable requires particular notice, āmīcītĭăm, which can only come from āmīcŭs, though were we to hear the trisyllable so pronounced, what an outcry would be raised against such a false quantity ! This is truly straining at a gnat, and swallowing a camel : āmīcŭs has only one false quantity, its sound and cadence are just as good as those of ārĭdŭs or cīvĭcŭs ; but āmīcītĭăm, with its two false quantities enhanced by our slurred and hurried utterance, has every defect in quantity, cadence, and articulation, that a word can well have : it is unfit for prose and verse, and most unfit for an hexameter : in ămīcītĭām, the long and short syllables are happily divided, the articulation easy and distinct, the cadence (that of a choriambus, with a preceding short syllable) of a very pleasing kind, and the word so pronounced perfectly suited to its place in the hexameter [r]. No one, I presume, will venture to maintain, in regard to these last, or to the numerous examples I have given, the old position, that their rhythm is improved by the accentual mode: and should it be suspected or insinuated that I had difficulty in getting so many examples, and must nearly have exhausted the stock, I can truly say, with respect to much the largest part of them, that I was puzzled how to choose between the numbers that offered themselves. I of course except hexameters with eight or nine feet, or as many trochees: that they should be rare, is not

---

[r] The difference in the manner of pronouncing this polysyllable by the English, Italian, and French, is considerable, especially by the French: we have just seen how it is pronounced by the English: I must add however to its cacophony, what exclusively belongs to us, the very inharmonious sound of *sh* which we give to *t* before an *i*. The Italians give to it that of *ts*, and I believe (for I speak with diffidence of any foreign pronunciation), pronouncing the word in the nominative, as in their own language they pronounce *amicizia*. On this, as on all other occasions, they are much more distinct in their articulation than we are, and give more length and force to the syllables which they pronounce as long; and therefore make cĭtĭăm, fully a dactyl. The French, I conceive, make but little difference in length or stress between the first four syllables, but give a decided length to the last, and perhaps give to the four first words a cadence like that of "Si pétulant en agitation:" while the cadence given by an Italian would be nearly "Si perfido nell' amicizia." As long as the Italians retain the accentual system, the very excellences of their utterance only serve to mark more distinctly the endless false quantities and errors of every kind to which it has given birth; were they guided by the ictus, those excellences would be displayed in a manner much more worthy of them, and with the fullest effect.

surprising; the wonder is, that they should exist. Still however it may be said, that there are not a few lines, the harmony of which, as they are usually pronounced, is universally admired, and would be greatly diminished were the quantity to be strictly observed. This last conclusion has I believe been always taken for granted : the truth of it has seldom if ever been fairly tried. Such a claim and assertion I have noticed, as having been made respecting hexameters of a particular structure, as ἔργα θέων-τα ρα-πάγχυ μάχης, and sácra cánunt-fu-némque mánu; and I then shewed what is obvious from the marks, that in our recitation the rhythm was as monotonous as the metre was false. I might be allowed to wait till some specific examples were proposed by the advocates of the system, as they would perhaps object to any that I myself should pitch upon : I will venture however to produce one which I think none of them will object to; for I have reason to think the rhythm of it, in our usual way of reciting it, is more admired for its beauty and harmony than almost any other, though most certainly the rules of ancient prosody are by no means strictly observed. It is the opening line of an admired simile in the fourth Georgic :

Quális populea moérens Philoméla sub umbra.

I readily allow that this set of words, as usually pronounced, has a pleasing cadence; but in the first three of them it no more belongs to the hexameter than to the iambic, alcaic, or any other metre. I shall begin by shewing why, in *spite* of the false quantities, not by *means* of them, the cadence is peculiarly pleasing to our ears : I speak however of the first part only, for that of the second, " Philoméla sub úmbra," is pleasing to every ear ; but it belongs to quantity, not to accent, to which the first part as exclusively belongs : and it is particularly necessary on this occasion to separate the properties. Of the three first words two are spondees, and those are made more agreeable to our taste, though they would not have been so to that of the spondaic Virgil, by being changed into trochees ; position stopping us as little in Latin as in English. The middle word is a choriambus of a very soft pleasing sound, pōpŭlĕă ; we change it as usual into a second peon, also of a very soft and pleasing sound, pŏpūlĕă, and one that is extremely familiar and agreeable to our ears, being the same as that of *Arcádia, Castália,* and other Anglicised words from the ancient languages : there are however two great objections to it ; one, that it is not, as we pronounce it, a Latin word, or probably a word in any language ; the other, that if it were, it would be inadmissible in that place.

The test I have more than once had recourse to, that of substituting words of the same *real* quantity, will, I believe, at once dissipate the illusion, as

Tále perícula mónte Philomela sub umbra.

You cannot endure it, though the rhythm is the very same ; but the substituted words have not the disguising mask of habit, and the sound of *pericula,* though far from inharmonious, is not so soft and liquid as the one you had been used to: and you *know* the quantity to be false, not only in recitation but in structure. On the other hand, if you put the false peon in the place of a real one, the rhythm is equally pleasing and satisfactory; as if, instead of " metuenda perícula pellit," you say " metuenda populea pellit," you only know on reflection that the real quantity is wrong. You would not like " quale propágine mira" better than " quale perícula;" but, at the end of an iambic, " adúlta vítium populea" does just as well for the rhythm as " vítium propágine;" and it so happens the substantive ends the next verse, which, to accord with our pronunciation of the adjective, ought to be pronounced ā'ltăs mărī'tăt pŏpū'lŏs. I must point my batteries against this favourite verse in every direction: suppose then a verse with a rhythm in the first hemistich, like that of " Et cum frigida mors;" as

Qua jam populus haec, moerensque Camilla sub umbra:

you would stare if any one were to read it,

Quā jăm pŏpūlŭs haēc, moērĕnsqŭe Cămīllă:

yet you will see by the marks that the quantity of all the syllables, and the rhythm that must accompany them, is the same, as in

Quālĭs pŏpūlĕă moērĕns Phĭlŏmēlă,

and that you cannot, if you observe the ancient marks, pronounce this last differently from, what you usually do, or the other differently from this.

N

Virgil seems to have intended this simile for a sort of θρῆνος, and to move on in a slow dirge-like strain: for this purpose he has employed, especially in the middle part, many spondees and molossi: the reader well knows the change we make in them, but probably has never thought of the number of long syllables that are shortened by such changes in the suite of four or five lines, and this is a very good opportunity of shewing it in particular lines, and in the amount altogether:

> Quālĭs pŏpūlĕă moērĕns Phĭlŏmēlă sŭb ūmbră
> Āmīssŏs qūerĭtŭr foētŭs, quŏs dūrŭs ărātŏr
> Ōbsērvăns nīdŏ ĭmplūmĕs dĕtrāxĭt: ăt īllă
> Flēt nōctĕm, rămōquĕ sēdĕns mĭsĕrābĭlĕ cārmĕn
> Īntĕgrăt, ĕt moēstĭs lātĕ lōcă quēstĭbŭs īmplĕt.

The opening verse is more flowing than any of the others; it has by quantity nine long syllables (six of them in the three first words), which we reduce to half their number, and six short ones; by accent there are six long, and nine short. The second verse, ten long, three short; by accent, six long, nine short. The third verse, eleven long, two short; by accent, six long, eight short. The whole number of long syllables by quantity, forty-eight; of short, twenty-three; by accent, of long, thirty; of short, forty-two. Were the accentual system to be put on its trial, and this one insulated fact to be stated (as I trust it now has been) on clear undeniable grounds, the court I think must be fully satisfied without any farther evidence, and at once pass sentence.

The present case is indeed a particularly strong one: metre and rhythm at all times obviously require that the long syllables should have their due length in recitation; but here the expression throughout requires that, instead of being curtailed or hurried over, they should seem to be more than usually dwelt on, and as if we wished to linger upon them. The attentive reader will have observed that three out of the five verses in the simile are headless, two of them beginning with a molossus, and the third with a monosyllable followed by a dissyllable.

I have shewn in various instances, that by avoiding to lay an accent on long finals, and being therefore obliged to shift it to some other syllable, we injure the sound and the articulation of the words, and in many cases their expression. With regard to this last, there is a very numerous set of words, both Greek and Latin, in which we uniformly injure it, and most essentially: these are compound words, chiefly molossi and choriambi, in which the additional syllable at the beginning either reverses, enforces, or in some way alters and modifies the sense of the simple. Such is the effect of the alpha privativum, and of the Latin *in;* and when the full length and stress are given to them, as ἀθανατους, *intrepidos,* we mark on the one the exemption from death, on the other from terror; but when the accent and stress are laid, as we lay them, on the second syllable, as ἀθἀ'νᾰτοῠς, *ĭntrē'pĭdŏs,* the privative is in both cases slightly passed over, and the simples, θᾰ'νᾰτοῠς and *trē'pĭdŭs* (for so we pronounce them) are alone brought into notice, and impressed on the ear; just as those of constancy and happiness are when we say *ĭn-cō'nstăns* and *ĭnfē'lĭx*. Other compounds again strongly enforce or extend the sense of the simple, as εχπερσαι, *evertens*; while others again fix and determine its general and vague meaning, as in the numerous compounds from the obsolete *specio*, as *aspicio*, *prospicio*, *despicio*, &c. In these, whenever the final is short, we very properly lay the accent on the first, as *ā'spĭcĕ*; but where it is long, never fail to shorten it, as in a line of Virgil's with plenty of elided *m's*:

Ăspē'ctăns sȳ'lvăm ĭmmē'nsăm, ĕt sĭc ō'rĕ prĕcā'tur:

and sometimes in words of four syllables, where the last is short, but elided; as

Dĕspī'cĕrĕ ū'ndĕ quēăs ā'lĭŏs, păssī'mquĕ vĭdē're.

In some cases the very look of the speaker is imaged to to us, and the true tone of the voice indicated by the emphatic addition; as in the affecting picture of Andromache, when she hears from the cold-blooded Æneas that unfeeling and unfounded reproach,

Hē'ctŏrĭs Ăndrō'măchĕ, Pȳ'rrhĭn' cŏ'nnū'bĭă sē'rvas?

Dĕjē'cĭt vū'ltŭm ĕt sŭbmī'ssă vō'cĕ lŏquūtă ēst.

In the second verse, the suite of eight long syllables was probably not unintentional; we shorten five, and among them *de* and *sub*. But are the emphatic syllables long in *all* compound words? the fact is notoriously otherwise; they are often, perhaps as often, short, as in ανωνυμος, απειρων, *inhospitus, inultus,* &c. &c. and it would be as flagrant a violation of the rules of prosody to increase their length, as to diminish that of the others. The question is not whether in all cases we are to make such emphatic syllables long, in order to give them their full expression, but whether, in the numerous cases where they *are* long, it be not, on every account, incumbent on us so to pronounce them, that they may lose nothing of their true character and effect. It would, as I have said, be a flagrant sin against prosody to lengthen the short emphatic syllables; but of the two sins, that of lengthening a short syllable, by which expression would be gained, is that which I be most inclined to forgive; and I may produce an instance or two where such forgiveness may be required. The two sorts of compounds sometimes occur in the same line, as

Αφρητωρ, αθεμιστος, ανεστιος εστιν εκεινος.

No one can doubt that the long α in the first word is more expressive of privation than the short α in the following words; yet there can be as little doubt, that after the long final τωρ, we are to pass rapidly over the two short syllables of αθεμιστος: but what is our practice? one that is worthy of our system; we shorten the first (as likewise the last) of αφρητωρ, and having shortened τωρ, are led to weigh too much on the first of αθεμιστος, and to turn the word into a favourite foot of our's, a ditrochee, preceded by an amphibrach, ἄφρή'τῶϱ ἄ'θἔμῖ'στὄς. We do the same, reversing the order, in a line of Virgil's:

Nŏs ā'nĭmaĕ vī'lĕs ī'nhŭmā'tă ĭnflē'tăquĕ tū'rba.

This is a sort of give and take: but as we deprive a long syllable of its rightful emphasis, which we bestow on a short one, and in both cases by means of a false quantity, it is a poor compensation.

It is thus that we have deprived a very numerous set of words in Greek and Latin, of an emphatic distinction at the beginning, by not laying an accent, where the sense and the quantity equally require it, on the *first* syllable: but, with regard to *distinction*, we do a much more extensive mischief by *not* laying it, in numberless instances, on the *last*; upon which the whole structure of those languages, as well as the rules of their prosody, require it to be laid. Throughout them both, the distinction of moods, tenses, cases, and persons, in verbs and in nouns, is chiefly made by the variations in the *final* syllable: the *first* in most instances remaining the same: these finals are generally long, or liable to be made so by position, as in the verb *paveo, paves, pavet, paveas;* or in the noun *pagus, pagi, pago, pagis, pagos*[a]. All these discriminating changes in the termination are at once felt, when the voice distinctly marks

---

[a] Schoolboys often make this distinction, from feeling that it ought to be made, and say, τυπτώ, τυπτείς, τυπτεί, bonús, boni, bonó, but on all other occasions relapse into the usual pronunciation.

and dwells upon them: *we* uniformly lay an accent on the unchanging first syllable, and go on, like children, crying *pa, pa, pa, pa,* throughout every conjugation and declension. When this does not make a positive false quantity, or an ambiguous sense, as it does in *véni, fúgit,* &c. it makes the sense much less clear and evident, and this alone is a great injury. Quantity is the true panacea on all such occasions; and if applied to the beginnings and the endings of these much injured verbs and nouns, it will at once cure the evil, and, if I may be allowed in this grave grammatical discussion to quote a ludicrous verse of Sir C. H. Williams,

'Twill set right their heads and their tails.

A monosyllable at the beginning of an hexameter, before a spondee, a pyrrhic, or an anapæst, has in our recitation nearly the same consequences; as in a line already quoted, *flĕt nō'ctĕm:* no one certainly will maintain, that, either for the metre or the expression, *flet* should be shortened and hurried over, or the spondee *nōctēm* should not, on the same account, have its full length: but the commonest monosyllables, from such a place in the verse, and often from a discriminating quality, strongly require the ictus, as

Nŏn qūíă Maĕcē'năs.
Hĭc gē'lĭdĭ fō'ntĕs, hĭc mō'llĭă prā'tă Lĭcō'ri,
Hĭc nē'mŭs, hĭc ī'psŏ tēcŭm cŏnsū'mĕrĕr āévo:

and such examples occur in every page. There are

many monosyllables so emphatic in their nature, especially at the beginning of a verse, that it is an absolute sin against expression to slur them over as we do so very frequently. Of that description is *nil;* and when at the beginning of an hexameter it receives the ictus, it seems to carry it on through the whole period as the sole emphatic word, whether used in the way of interrogation, as

Nĭl ḗrgŏ ŏptā̆bŭnt hō'mĭnĕs? sĭ cōnsĭ'lĭŭm vĭ's,

(a verse, by the bye, to which, as well as to the one that follows it, accent has the exclusive right); or of strong position and assertion, as in another well known verse of Juvenal:

Nĭl hā̆'bĕt ĭnfē̆'lĭx paŭpē̆'rtăs dū̆'rĭŭs ĭn sē̄'
Quā̆'m quŏd rĭdĭ'cŭlŏs hō'mĭnĕs fā̆'cĭt;

or again in a verse in Lucan, of great notoriety:

Nĭl ā̆'ctŭm rē̆'pŭtăns dŭm quĭ'd sŭpĕrē̆'ssĕt ăgē̄'ndŭm.

There are some monosyllables expressive of motion usually connected with rapidity, and therefore at the beginning of a verse very much require, what they have so good a right to, the ictus metricus; as,

βᾰν ῥ' ἴμ̆εν· ἤρχε δ' ἄρᾰ σφῐ Πο̆'σειδᾰ'ων Ε̄'νοσῐ'χθων.

In the first part of this verse the dactylic rapidity is

completely checked by ῥ᾽ ἵμεν and δ᾽ ἄρα, and the striking grandeur in sound and cadence of the two proper names made almost burlesque by the two chiming ditrochees, Πό᾽σε̆ῐδᾰ᾽ῶν Ἐ᾽νο̆σῐ᾽χθῶν. Βασκε is another such word always joined with ἴθἳ, and of course a dactyl, as in a line already quoted:

$$\beta\breve{a}\sigma\varkappa' \; \breve{\imath}'\theta\breve{\imath} \; \bar{I}'\varrho\breve{\imath} \; \tau\breve{a}\chi\bar{e}\breve{\imath}\breve{a}, \; \pi\breve{a}'\lambda\breve{\imath}\nu \; \tau\varrho\bar{e}'\pi\breve{e}, \; \mu\breve{\eta}\delta' \; \bar{e}'\breve{a} \; \breve{a}'\nu\tau\eta\nu.$$

The marks above and below are a sufficient comment. But there are monosyllables to which length and stress seem so attached, that nothing but the perverseness of our system, and our blind obedience to it, could ever have deprived them of those qualities: I particularly allude to the interjections Ω and O, as they are variously applied to eager expostulation, admiration, lamentation, to earnest wishes and regrets, &c. Ω is frequently joined to μοι, in which case we always lay the accent where the ictus is, on the Ω, as Ώ' μοι Τύδεος υἱε, but where μοι does not follow Ω, we perpetually disjoin the accent from the ictus, as in

$$\breve{\Omega} \; \bar{A}'\chi\breve{\imath}\lambda\varepsilon\breve{\upsilon} \; \mu\breve{a}'\lambda\breve{a} \; \sigma\breve{o}\breve{\imath} \; \varkappa\bar{e}\chi\breve{o}\lambda\bar{\omega}'\sigma\breve{o}\mu\alpha\breve{\imath}, \; \breve{a}\breve{\imath}\varkappa\bar{e} \; \tau\bar{e}\lambda\bar{e}'\sigma\eta\varsigma$$
$$\text{T}\breve{o}\acute{u}\tau\breve{o} \; \bar{e}'\pi\breve{o}\varsigma^{t}.$$

---

[t] Those who do not remember whence this line is taken, and the circumstances that gave rise to the expostulation, and *do* remember from Patroclus's account οἷος ἐκεῖνος Δεῖνος ἀνηρ, may wonder who the person is that ventured to tell Achilles how angry he shall be with him, if he does what he intends doing. There is in the style of the expostulation, and of the whole of what comes afterwards, a sort of frank, animated, juvenile familiarity, that can suit no one but Antilochus, the youthful and amiable friend

And again where Priam, struck with Agamemnon's appearance, and with Helen's account of his great qualities, exclaims,

Ὦ μά'κᾰρ Ἀτρε'ΐδῆ, μοΐρῆ'γἔνἕς, ὅ'λβΐοδαΐμων.

In the Lavacrum Palladis of Callimachus the ω is used three times in the same distich, as an interjection of grief and lamentation: it is where the mother of Tiresias, seeing her son struck blind, exclaims,

Εῖδἕς Ἀ'θῆναι'ῆς στῆ'θἔᾰ κᾱι λᾰ'γὄνᾱς·

Ἄλλ' ὄύκ ῆἕ'λΐὄν πᾱ'λῖν ὄ'ψἕαῖ· ὤ ἔ'μἔ δεῖλᾰν,

Ὦ ὅ'ρῦς, ὤ Ἑ'λῖκῶν, ὄύκ ἔ'τῖ μὄι πᾱ'ρῖτἔ.

As I have put down a line and a half for the sense and connection, I will first notice the ditrochee Ἀθῆναΐῆς instead of the first epitrite Ἄθῆναῖῆς, so well suited to metre, rhythm, and to the dignity of the goddess : and also, what is more to the present purpose, the shorten-

---

of the great hero; who, delighted with his spirit, smiles at his request, and immediately grants it :

'Ὡς φάτο· μειδήσεν δε ποδάρκης δῖος Ἀχίλλευς,

Χαίρων Ἀντίλοχῳ ὅτι οἱ φίλος ἤεν ἑταίρος.

There is something very delightful in seeing the fierce Achilles, the most terrible of men, good-naturedly smiling; and throughout this twenty-third book doing the honours of the games with a nobleness of manner, a kindness of feeling, and a delicacy of attention, that seem to belong to him as truly as the more imposing parts of his character. Perhaps the greatest charm of the most sublime of all the ancient poets, is a variety and discrimination of manner and character, in which Shakespear is his only rival.

ing of the disjunctive αλλ'; as to the main point, the ω, we shorten and slur it over each time, and each time give length and stress to an ε or an ο.

In Virgil's ninth Eclogue, of grief and indignation:

Ŏ Lȳ′cĭdă, vī′vĭ pĕrvē′nĭmŭs, ā′dvĕnă nōstris.

In the first Æneid (l. 202), of kindness and encouragement:

Ŏ sō′cĭĭ nɘ′quĕ ē′nĭm ĭgnā′rĭ sū′mŭs ā′ntĕ mălō′rum,

Ŏ pā′ssĭ grăvĭō′ră; dā′bĭt D 'ŭs hĭs quō′quĕ fī′nem.

In the second Æneid, of affection and consolation:

Ŏ dū′lcĭs cō′njŭx? nŏn hāec sī′nĕ nū′mĭnĕ Dī′vum

Ēvē′nĭŭnt.

Of shame and self reproach:

Ὦ Κῡ′κλῶψ Κῡ′κλῶψ, πᾷ τόί φρε̆′νε̆ς έκπε̆πότα′ται.

Ŏ Cō′rȳdŏn, Cŏ′rȳdŏn, quāē tĕ dĕmē′ntĭă cē′pit?

Of sarcasm:

Ŏ qūălĭs fā′cĭĕs ĕt qūălĭ dī′gnă tăbē′llă!

Of grave and indignant satire:

Ŏ cāecăs hō′mĭnŭm mē′ntĕs! Ŏ pē′ctŏră vā′na!

Of reproach, as of Turnus and Juturna:

Ŏ sō′rŏr ĕt dū′dŭm ăgnō′vĭ quŭm prī′mă pĕr ā′rtem.

This last line consists wholly of amphibrachs; the next of comic exclamation, when we consider the subject of the lines, and the person they are addressed to:

Ŏ rḗm rĭdĭ'cŭlăm Cā'tŏ ĕt jŏcō'săm.

Of frank and hearty contempt:

Tḗcŭm Lḗsbĭă nō'stră cō'mpărē'tŭr?

Ŏ sāéclŭm ĭnsĭ'pĭĕns ĕt ĭ'nvĕnū'stum.

These examples, all of them beginning with a long *O*, are very numerous and diversified; yet I am apt to think that a good reciter would, in a large portion of them, be able to make such a distinction between the different sounds of the *O*, according to the particular expression, that an intelligent hearer would readily perceive it: he of course must observe the ictus; for unless the full length and stress be given to the vowel, no skill could produce the effect; and our mode, together with metre and rhythm, has destroyed even the means of giving the true, full, and varied expression. There are other interjections, as αιθε in Greek, and *heu!* in Latin, that we use much in the same way, as

Αἴθ' οὑτῶς ἔπῒ πᾶσῖ χο'λὸν τὲλἔσεῖ' Ἀ'γᾰμἔ'μνῶν.

Ὡς ο'φἔλἔν θᾱ'νᾰτὄς μοῖ ἀ'δεῖν κᾰ'κὄς, 'ὄ'ππὄτἔ δεύρο.

Heŭ pĭ'ĕtăs, heŭ prĭ'scă fĭ'dĕs, ĭnvĭ'ctăquĕ bē'llo.

I lastly come to a set of monosyllables, that no less

require length and stress than the interjections, and are
no less deprived of both by our mode ; I mean the pro-
nouns *me, nos, tu, te, vos;* as,

Mĕ fā′mŭlăm fămŭlō′quĕ Hē′lĭnŏ trănsmī′sĭt hăbē′ndăm ;

or, as it not unfrequently happens, when any of them
are opposed to each other, and when the *ictus* requires
to be more particularly marked, as,

Tŭ gē′nĭtŏr cā′pĕ sä′cră mā′nŭ, pătrĭō′squĕ pĕnā′tĕs;

Mĕ bē′llŏ ă tā′ntŏ dĭgrē′ssŭm ĕt cāédĕ rĕcē′ntĭ

Ā′ttrĕctā′rĕ nē′făs.

Vŏs fā′mŭlĭ quaĕ dī′căm ā′nĭmĭs ădvē′rtĭtĕ vē′stris.

Tŭ rē′quĭĕs mĭ′sĕrĭs, dē′cŭs īmpĕrĭūmquĕ Lătĭ′ni

Tĕ pē′nĕs ;

Tŭ lā′crўmĭs ĕvĭ′ctă mē′ĭs, tŭ prī′mă fŭrē′ntem.

Tŭ vē′rŏ dŭbĭtā′bĭs ĕt ĭ′ndĭgnā′bĕrĕ ŏbī′rĕ ?

In a very affecting distich of Tibullus, *Te* is used at
the beginning of each line : and I think there are few
readers, however fond of the old method, who will not
feel the extreme difference in the expression when it has
and when it has not the ictus :

Tĕ spē′ctĕm sŭprē′mă mĭ′hĭ cŭm vē′nĕrĭt hō′ră,

Tĕ tĕ′nĕăm mō′rĭĕns dē′fĭcĭē′ntĕ mā′nŭ.

Affection, in addressing the beloved object, naturally

pronounces such words as *tu* or *te* in a somewhat fuller
or more elevated and impressive tone, than any in other
parts of that verse and passage : certainly would not
slur over them, in order to dwell upon *spec;* and when
resting upon sad and mournful images, the words move
slow, and so they must according to the structure of
the hexameter ; for in the four first words there are six
long syllables (five of them in succession), and the feet
two spondees and a choriambus, Tē spēctēm sūprēmă
mĭhĭ, and they are well suited to the longing lingering
look : in our mode, the five successive long syllables are
reduced to two ; the iambus *mĭhī*, on the final of which
the voice drops, has the quantity reversed ; and nothing
could be invented more ill-suited to the expression than
two jigging amphibrachs followed by a trochee, Tĕ
spēctĕm sŭprēmă mĭhĭ. The first hemistich of the
pentameter has only three long syllables, but two of
them are the finals of anapæsts, which, though rapid
feet, are, on account of their finals, better suited to the
subject than dactyls, as *tēnĕăm* and *mŏrĭĕns*. To the
enormous and crying sin of shortening the *te*, must be
added the peccadillo of a jingle produced by it on *te te*
in Tĕ tē-nĕăm. I will give one more example of *te :*
it is from the beginning of Lucretius, where, in his
beautiful address to Venus, it is used three times in one
line :

Tĕ, dē'ă̱, tĕ fū'gĭŭnt vē'ntĭ̱, tĕ nū'bĭlă cōéli.

In the first and second the ictus only is on *te;* the
third time it is, with the accent, on *nu.* The dif-

ference, as I have before observed, and here think it right to repeat, is, that the accent being on *nu*, the *te* becomes short; but it remains long *though* the ictus is on another syllable, and from its length admits of a subordinate stress being laid on it, which cannot be done in the other case. This beautiful verse and image Dryden has very happily introduced into our poetry, in his Palamon and Arcite, preserving, as much as the difference of language and metre would allow him, the character and cadence of the original:

> Thee, goddess, thee the storms of winter fly.

I will now make the same change in the quantities or accents (no matter by which name they are called) of the English verse that we make in the Latin one, having just as good a right to do so:

> Tĕ dēă tĕ fūgĭŭnt vēntĭ.
>
> Theĕ, gōddĕss, theĕ thē stŏrms ŏf wīntĕr.

Although we are persuaded that the rhythm of the Latin verse is improved by the false quantities, no one, I believe, will think that of the English one improved by the same panacea; perhaps from the dose not being strong enough; for in the Latin one, as far as I have gone, and till you get to the adonic, every word contains a false quantity; whereas *gōddĕss* and *wīntĕr* retain the true; and if *thē stŏrms ŏf* should be thought a reluctant dactyl, we have some such in common use, as *mĭ'nstrĕlsў*, *Brō'bdĭgnăg*, and, what would sound most strange to an ancient Greek or Roman, *chă'răctĕr*, from χᾰρᾰκτῆρ.

The rhythm of the Latin line to the adonic is, as we pronounce it, neither that of an hexameter, nor of any other metre; but (what shews the pertinacity of ancient prosody, and the pliability of our's) the English line, when completely taken out of the heroic metre, is transformed into another, the same as " three goddesses standing together." The last example of this kind that I shall give is from Virgil's first eclogue, the opening line of which,

Tǐtȳrě tǔ pā'tǔlaě rē'cǔbăns sǔb tē'gmǐně fā'gi,

is perhaps the most familiar to us of any ancient poetry, and is almost as strongly marked as any with the vices of accentual pronunciation. It is in the first place one of our bastard pentameters; the four words, *Tityre, pátulae, récubans*, and *tégmine*, are all accented alike, all equally dactyls; and, what is to the point in question, the highly emphatic monosyllable *tu* is shortened and slurred over: the mere circumstance of making any syllable short after a complete foot, is, next to that of making it short at the beginning of an hexameter, one of the most heinous sins against metre, and greatly aggravated when the syllable is emphatic. This is a large set of enormities in a single verse, and there are several more of equal magnitude in the lines that follow, one especially relating to an emphatic monosyllable, which from its connection with *tu*, and its being strikingly opposed to it, makes the case altogether peculiarly impressive. In the five opening lines of the earliest production of the great Latin poet, the interest arises from the strongly marked contrast between the happiness and security of Tityrus, and the forlorn condition and sad prospects of Meliboeus and his companions in misfortune: the marks will clearly shew where the contrast is expressed and enforced, and where it is sunk and lost in recitation:

Tītўrĕ, tŭ pătŭlaĕ rēcŭbăns sŭb tēgmĭnĕ fāgĭ

Sўlvēstrĕm tēnŭĭ mūsăm mĕdĭtārĭs ăvēnă :

Nŏs pātrĭaĕ fīnĕs, ĕt dūlcĭă līnquĭmŭs ārvă ;

Nŏs pātrĭăm fŭgĭmŭs : tŭ, Tītўrĕ, lēntŭs ĭn ūmbră

Fŏrmōsăm rĕsŏnārĕ dōcĕs Ămărўllĭdă sўlvăs.

When we observe the ictus and quantity, there are six legitimate feet; spondees and iambi are distinguished from trochees; anapæsts from dactyls; molossi from amphibrachs; and above all, the emphatic words *tu* and *nos* have their due length and consequence. It might be said, however, by an advocate for the system, and indeed has been said, " I allow that we lay an accent on the first of *pátulae* and *pátriae,* and do not lay one on *tu* and *nos,* and generally make them short; but we *can* give them length and stress, and a judicious reader, for the sake of the expression, would do so." He would do right as far as these words were concerned, but wrong in respect to his system and its rules, one of which is, that all unaccented syllables should be quickly passed over to the next accented one : on this rule depends the flow of rhythm, such as it is, so highly rated, for it is checked and clogged when an unaccented syllable is pronounced long,·as " Tī'tўrĕ tū pā'tŭlaĕ," and there is comparatively no effect; whereas in the structure of the verse, and in the recitation as guided by the ictus, *tu* is in the best possible situation for the purpose of effect, for it comes immediately after and before two short syllables, Tītўrĕ-tū-pătŭlaē. In the accentual pronunciation, an effort is required to make *tu* long, against the rules and the usual practice; in the recitation by the ictus there is no effort, every thing is in its natural place, and it would require an effort, and a most unnatural one, to make the syllable short.

I have constantly, as the reader has seen, placed the ancient mark of long where we lay our accent, and the mark of short where we do not lay it; and should think myself fully justified in doing so by the authority of Johnson and Foster, and, if I may be allowed to say so, by some additional arguments and illustrations of my own, supposing I had been the first who had ventured on such a practice; but I had a precedent, which it is right to mention, as the person I allude to has plainly shewn, that in his opinion the Italians consider their accent as lengthening any Latin syllable on which it may be placed, however short, and shortening any on which it is *not* placed, however long: and on this particular point I should think his opinion may be relied upon, whatever may be the case on others; especially as, according to his account, the Italian mode of accenting the Latin is precisely the same with our's, as likewise the result in respect to quantity; a coincidence which could not well take place if there were any thing false in his or in my statement. The person I alluded to in a former part is the Abbate Scoppa, by birth a Sicilian; his work was crowned by the French Institute *et pour cause*, is written in French; the title of it, a most comprehensive one, and implying a thorough acquaintance with the languages of all ages and countries, is, " Des Beautés Poétiques de toutes les Langues." Upon looking into the work, however, we find that *toutes* means *trois :* Italian, French, and Latin, the only languages with which he appears to have been much, if at all, acquainted. He deserved his crown, for he speaks in the most flattering terms of the French language, and particularly (who could have suspected it?) of the charm of their *e muet*. The English, Germans, Spaniards, Portuguese, &c. might feel a little mortified at being considered as having no languages, or, at least, such as are destitute of any poetical beauties, were it not that the language of Homer, " a quo ceu fonte perenni, &c." has as little share in this *ouvrage couronné*. The Abbate's great point is to establish by arguments and examples, what is but too firmly established in practice, the preeminence of accent over quantity; as mine is to subvert it, and restore what I conceive to be the true and lawful preeminence of quantity [u]. His position, like that of persons of the

[u] Dr. Warner gives the following account of a conversation he had at Rome with a learned ecclesiastic. They were walking together in the Campo Vaccino, the ancient Forum and Via Sacra; and the spot putting them in mind of Horace and his adventure, his companion began repeating

same persuasion in this country, is, in his own words,
" lisez tous les vers de Virgile, d'Horace en altérant
exprès toutes les quantités prosodiques, mais en re-
spectant constamment le ton et les percussions de l'accent tonique: vous trouverez dans la déclamation de
ces vers une harmonie ravissante. Tout au contraire
déclamez ces mêmes vers, en observant autant que possible les quantités prosodiques, mais en changeant toujours les places principales des accens aigus ; vous
trouverez que ces vers restent tout-a-fait denués d'harmonie." He has put down, but in another part, a suite
of ten hexameters with the ancient marks of long where
the Romans laid their acute, and of short on the syllables not acuted. I shall put them all down as a curious
specimen of such a number of barefaced and avowed
false quantities ; not, like those I have given, in order
to deter the reader by their deformity, but to allure
him by their happy effect on the rhythm, and confirm
him in the practice :

" Ibam forte via sacra," but according to the true quantity. This mode of
pronouncing, perfectly new to Dr. Warner, very much surprised and
pleased him ; when the Italian, entering upon the subject, mentioned
various objections to the English mode of accenting the Latin, in which, he
observed to the Doctor, you are more or less countenanced by the generality
of my countrymen. The whole passage, which begins in page 11. of
Metronariston, is too long for insertion ; but if Dr. Warner's account be
exact, and I know of no reason for thinking otherwise, it clearly shews,
that the true quantity was at that time observed by *some* Italians: and
perhaps the case may now be in Italy not very different from what it is in
England, a general compliance with the established usage, and a strong
conviction, among many reflecting minds, of its complete absurdity.

Vūlnŭs ālĭt vēnĭs ĕt caēcŏ cārpĭtŭr īgni.

Ànnă sŏrŏr, quāe mĕ. sŭspēnsăm ĭnsōmnĭă tērrent.

Nŏs pātrĭaĕ fīnĕs ĕt dūlcĭă līnquĭmŭs ārva.

Quĭs fūrŏr ŏ cīvĕs? quāe tāntă lĭcēntĭă fērri ?

Ĭn sŭă vĭctrīcĭ cŏnvērsŭm vīscĕră dēxtra.

Quĭs nŏvŭs hĭc nōstrĭs sŭccēssĭt sēdĭbŭs hōspes ?

Ĕt sōl crēscēntĕs dĕcēdĕns dūplĭcăt ūmbras.

Mīllĕ mēaĕ Sīcŭlĭs ērrănt ĭn mōntĭbŭs āgni.

Ārmă vĭrūmqŭe cānŏ Trōjaĕ qŭi prīmŭs ăb ōris.

Āt rĕgīnă grăvĭ jămdūdŭm sāucĭă cūra.

He then says, " l'oreille sent dans la distribution de ces
pieds une percussion vers la fin, une harmonie parfaite :
elle sent que dans chaque vers hexamétre on ne frappe
plus six fois; elle n'y compte évidemment que cinq
coups, cinq vibrations, cinq percussions, c'est à dire cinq
pieds." My first remark on the ten lines (which probably some of my readers may have anticipated) is,
that in all of them the adonics are pronounced according
to quantity; and the ear being pleased and satisfied at
the close, is disposed to forget whatever may have been
wrong in the earlier part. Of this the Abbate seems to
have been aware, for he has carefully selected such lines
to the exclusion of all others; and from the expression
" une percussion *vers la fin,* une harmonie parfaite," he
appears to have trusted very much to the adonic. He
appears likewise to have been aware that redundant
syllables, which we pronounce in Latin, are not favourable to harmony; and accordingly there is only one

elision in the ten lines. The Italians, I may venture to
say, have always, like the English (who, I have no
doubt, took the present mode from them, *tale quale*),
been used to consider the cadence of all Latin verses
that pleased their ears, as produced by the accentual
system, and as a proof of its excellence; and no one, I
believe, ever thought of considering what part of the
cadence belonged to accent and what to quantity : the
adonics therefore have always been given to accent;
ἀταϱ ην ποτε δασμος ἰκηται, it will be found that they,
and whatever is truly harmonious and congenial to
metre, belong to quantity; and when the pure ore is
separated from the dross, what remains will be dross
indeed.   I have already made that separation in numerous instances, but they certainly were not selected as
favourable to accent : the ten lines were carefully selected with that view, and it will be but fair to try on
part of them the same experiment in the same manner
by means of the ictus :

> Vūlnŭs ālĭt vēnĭs ĕt caēcŏ-cārpĭtŭr īgni.
>
> Nŏs pātrĭaĕ fīnĕs ĕt-dūlcĭă līnquĭmŭs ārva.
>
> Quĭs fūrŏr ŏ cīvĕs? quaĕ-tāntă lĭcēntĭă fērri.
>
> Ĕt sōl crĕscēntĕs dĕcēdĕns-dūplĭcăt ūmbras.

Such false quantities, as ŏ, *crĕscēntĕs, dĕcēdĕns*, and in
another way, as *fūrŏr, sūă, mēaĕ*, &c. make a strange
appearance; but in respect to them, we have in the
Abbate, not merely *confitentem*, but *gloriantem reum ;*

and though he does not, as far as I remember, profess his disregard for metre, yet no one can have any regard for it who has a contempt for the *quantités prosodiques*: my remarks then shall be confined to rhythm. In the first line there are three successive trochees, and an amphibrach, *ĕt caēcŏ*; the most monotonous rhythm opposed to the most varied, as it is shewn by the ictus. In the first hemistich of the second line I should think the choriambus, *nos patriae*, would, merely for the rhythm, and not considering the emphatic word, and its expression, be preferred to *nŏs pātriaĕ*: the whole of the second hemistich is remarkably sweet and pleasing, but, as accent and ictus coincide, belongs solely to quantity. The third line is a succession of amphibrachs, but the adonic and the dactyl before it belong to quantity. The fourth line begins (oddly enough for an hexameter) with an iambus, and that a very odd one, *ĕt sōl*, which is succeeded by two as strange amphibrachs, *crĕscēntĕs* and *dĕcēdĕns*; the rhythm, such as it is, belongs, I believe, to no metre whatever, and a pity it should. The Abbate gives a decided preference to the anapæst and the anapæstic rhythm to the dactyl and the dactylic, and, like St. Austin, is for reciting hexameters by anapæsts and spondees, instead of dactyls and spondees. I have slightly touched upon this point, and have shewn how much, in some cases, the anapæstic rhythm is to be preferred for the expression, in others the dactylic; but I very strongly object to any exclusive adoption or rejection, and especially, if I understand it rightly, to the mode which is proposed,

that of disjoining the two short syllables of the dactyl
from the preceding long one, in order to join them to a
succeeding long syllable as anapæsts. Thus, instead of
the very flowing and continued rhythm of *dúlcia lín-
quimus árva*, we should have *dūl-cĭă līn-quĭmŭs ār-;* as
to *va*, it would be left *sola soletta*, and, as we shall soon
see, might think itself lucky to be left at all. The odd
thing is, and really most singularly perverse, that when
there is an anapæst in the verse, which, when pronounced as such, makes the verse begin with a long
syllable, and one of so much consequence-*nos patriam,*
it is changed into what these exclusive lovers of anapæsts wish to avoid- a dactyl; and in the next line two
of them are changed in the same manner, *nŏs pātrĭăm
fŭgĭmŭs!* in short, the anapæst so praised is absolutely
abolished in recitation, *laudandus tollendus,* and a set
of spurious dactyls substituted in its room. I have
strongly reprobated any excess or diminution in regard
to the six feet of the hexameter: the Abbate, on the
other hand, is quite vain of having, in all the ten lines,
reduced them to five, and weighs upon it with great
earnestness: " cinq coups, cinq vibrations, cinq percussions, c'est à dire, cinq pieds :" and even this, which there
is so little reason to be proud of, is not true; for in
each of the two first lines there are evidently six accented syllables, and therefore six percussions:

Vúlnus | álit | vénis | et caéco | cárpitur | ígni,
A'nna | sóror | quaé me | suspénsam | insómnia | térrent.

And it is the same with the eighth and the tenth verse:

if he chose to be vain on such an occasion, he should at least have been accurate.

In order to shew fairly its beneficial effects in regard to rhythm, the accentual system ought to operate throughout the whole, or, at least, the greatest part of the verse. I will now do what the Abbate has not done (I will not say has neglected to do), by putting down four verses, with the first part nearly like the four I have taken from the ten, but with the last part of a very different cadence:

Tēnĕ māgĭs sālvŭm pōpŭlŭs vēlĭt ăn pōpŭlŭm tū.
Rĕs Dānăŭm ; frāctaĕ vīrĕs, ăvērsă Dēaĕ mēns.
Tĕ sēquŏr ŏ Grāiaĕ gēntĭs dēcŭs ĭnquĕ tŭĭs nūnc.
Nĭl ērgŏ ŏptābŭnt hōmĭnĕs ? sĭ cŏnsĭlĭŭm vīs.

What a difference when there is no smoothly flowing adonic to relieve and comfort the reader and hearer at the end of the verse! when, after all the false quantities, and consequently false cadences, in the earlier part, there is a continuation of them, and of the very worst kind, quite to the last syllable! I shall make but few remarks on these lines; the first however requires some: it is supposed to have been inserted by Horace in one of his epistles, from a poem addressed by Varius to Augustus: the rhythm of it consequently could not have been displeasing to the nicest ears in that best age of Latin poetry; and I may therefore safely assert, that the verse could not have been pronounced as we pronounce it, nor in any way at all approaching to it : but

there is another objection to our mode in this instance,
which may have weight with those who have little or no
regard to quantity and metre, or even to rhythm—that
of ambiguity. The sense of the entire passage, as we
pronounce the words, is, " may Jupiter, who watches
over you and the city of Rome, keep it doubtful whether the poplar is most anxious for your safety, or you
for the poplar's." If we could suppose an ancient
Roman, who happened not to be acquainted with the
passage, to have heard the verse recited as we recite it,
his first surprise would have been at the strange sort of
prose, for he could not have suspected it to be verse ;
and his next puzzle, who could be the person for whose
welfare the tree was so extremely anxious, and who was
not less so for that of the tree ; and he might perhaps
think of Hercules, to whom the poplar was sacred ; for
as to the Roman people, *pōpŭlŭs* could never make him
think of it : the fact is, that the sole distinction between
two words composed of the same letters, but with such
very different meanings, was the *quantity*, the *accent*
(the ancient acute) being equally on the first syllable of
them both. On that therefore the pitch of the voice
was always raised, but it must have been pronounced
long or short according to its sense :

Pō'pŭlŭs Alcidae gratissima, vitis Iaccho.

Tene magis salvum pŏ'pŭlūs velit, an pŏ'pŭlūm tu.

This circumstance of ambiguity will by many be
thought the strongest, perhaps the only strong, argu-

ment against reading by accent; but what argument could be wanting in addition to the plain statement, that these are two distinct feet, so much so, that the one is the exact reverse of the other, and therefore could never have been pronounced alike ; that the distinct pronunciations agree with the rules of prosody, the structure of verses, the guidance of the ictus, and are likewise required for the essential purpose of variety : this would have been more than sufficient without the ambiguity, as the ambiguity alone would have been without any thing else. What on the other side could be opposed to all or any part of this? nothing but the bare fact—which no one denies, but from which no inference respecting quantity, that has the slightest foundation, can be drawn—that the Romans laid their acute on the first of both feet. I have quoted only four lines belonging to accent, as judging them, after all that at various times had been said on the subject, enough for my purpose: the Abbate himself, I believe, had he recited them, *a modo suo*, would hardly have thought them " d'une harmonie ravissante," and might perhaps have secretly thought, had he condescended to try the experiment, that when recited according to the guidance of the ictus, and of the " quantités prosodiques," they were by no means " denués de toute harmonie :" I could easily have furnished him with ten times as many of the same sort. Although the smooth flow of adonics can cover, to our ears at least, many sins in the other parts of the verse, yet the sins are often of so flagrant a sort, that the ears of Midas could scarcely endure them, especially where there are several elisions, as

Ăntēvĕnĭ ĕt sōbŏlĕm ărmēntŏ sŏr-tire quotannis.

Praĕcīpŭŭm jăm īndĕ ă tēnĕrĭs ĭm-pende laborem.

Hĭnc quōquĕ ūbĭ aŭt mōrbŏ grāvĭs aūt jăm-segnior aetas.

To these three lines of Virgil, and from his most finished work, I will add one from Horace: it is thus that we recite his beautiful and feeling apostrophe to the country :

Ŏ rūs͵quāndŏ ēgŏ tĕ ăspĭcĭăm? quăn-doque licebit.

Observe now the extreme difference both in the rhythm and the expression with the ictus, and the consequent and necessary omission of the redundant syllables :

O rus͵quand' ego t' aspiciam? quandoque licebit.

In speaking of the recitation by anapæsts in lieu of dactyls, and of the concluding spondee being reduced to a single syllable, I intimated that the syllable was in some danger of being totally omitted ; and I alluded to a position of the Abbate Scoppa's, who is a great curtailer of what he chooses to consider as redundancies. He gives it as his decided opinion, " que tous les vers héroiques garderaient toujours leur harmonie naturelle en les prononçant sans la derniére syllabe :

Tītўrĕ tŭ pātŭlaĕ rēcŭbăns sŭb tēgmĭnĕ fa."

I must own I am for keeping the line—Virgil having written it so—with what the Abbate jocosely calls " une queue superflue :" for on this occasion nothing can be more strictly true than Voltaire's witty line :

Le superflus, chose très necessaire.

As the Abbate, whatever might have been his secret wish, does not propose to cut off the tails of all hexameters, but only to shew how well they would look without them, little more need be said : I will only add, that if I were obliged to part with one, it should be in the first line of the Æneid, but with a proviso that the true quantity should be kept ; for it then would make a remarkably pretty leonine verse :

Arma virumque cano, Trojae qui primus ab o.

The Abbate Scoppa's is the first and the only work in which I have seen accented syllables marked as long, and unaccented as short ; not, as I have done it, for the purpose of shewing the deformity of the system, but for that of pointing out its excellence. This certainly is a very open and explicit way of proceeding ; but, in an advocate, not perhaps a very prudent one : the relation between modern accent and quantity had been left undefined, and a sort of mysterious covering drawn over the whole ; till the Abbate, with a rash hand, " squarciò 'l velame ;" and now these glaring false quantities, which every one commits, and no one is willing to acknowledge, appear in their own proper shape, and boldly stare us in the face.

IN the preceding pages I have laid the main stress on the restoration of quantity, that of metre and of the genuine rhythm necessarily accompanying it : if to those essential points we were to add the Italian sound of the vowels, and the Italian utterance, we should attain, in the recitation of Greek and Latin verses, nearly all that, with our means, is attainable [x]. With this we must, and well may, be content; " le reste est un vain songe ;" for the idea of restoring, to any good purpose, ancient accent, though warmly entertained by several learned and ingenious persons, is, in my mind, little better than a fond dream. I have made use of the word *ancient*, but the great advocates for restoring accent, Sheke and Smith in the earlier, Foster and Horsley in the later times, do not seem to have had a thought of restoring it in Latin, and have entirely passed it over. The omission would however give rise to a dilemma in various ways : it would be strange if we were to recite Homer, raising our voices on the acutes, lowering them on the graves, and managing the circumflexes as well as we could, yet to recite Virgil without any of these regular elevations, depressions, and circumbendibus. On the

[x] The Italians, there is reason to suppose, give the same sound to the vowels as was given to them by the Romans, who probably pronounced all of them except the *u* nearly as the Greeks did their's. The upsilon was certainly pronounced differently from the Roman or the Italian *u;* what the pronunciation was, it may be difficult to ascertain ; on the sound of the ancient vowels and diphthongs I may hereafter have some remarks to offer.

other hand, were we to study both accentuations, the difficulty of the task would be greatly increased, the character of each being so different; and it would require a constant attention to keep the accents distinct, the feet and the metres being the same in both languages. But admitting (I need not say for argument's sake) that we had completely overcome all difficulties, had learnt to manage the Greek accents like any ancient Greek, the Latin like any old Roman, and without ever mixing or confounding them, the balance between the two languages, which leans towards the Greek, would be entirely destroyed. Homer's and Virgil's hexameters are now thought to be nearly on a par; Virgil's perhaps, in general, the greater favourites; but the language in which Homer's are written, avowedly more harmonious in its structure and cadence, had also, as we learn from an equally competent and impartial judge, a mode of accenting the most varied and flexible; while the inferiority of that in which Virgil wrote was increased by the rigidity and monotony of the accentuation. Now if the contrast was so striking to Quintilian, whom early and constant habit might be supposed to have reconciled to his own mode, or even to have prejudiced in its favour, what must it be to us, who, instead of having any favourable impressions from Roman habits, are prejudiced the other way by the judgment of such a Roman! were we then to recite Homer's verses with the true Greek accent, and then Virgil's (he is in no great danger either way) with the true Latin one, we might be led to say, like an eminent

Italian painter on a different occasion, " il quale prima mi pareva un miracolo, e adesso mi pare una cosa di legno, tanto dura e tagliente^y;" and this sort of stiff, unblending, wooden effect must have been that of the Latin, compared with the Greek accents. Quintilian, I suspect, would have been very glad to reverse what we, in our sense of the word, have done; namely, to apply the Greek accentuation to the Latin language: we perhaps might have no scruple on the subject, and no objection to carry into practice what I have supposed to be his wish; and it would completely get rid of this last part of the dilemma, and place the Latin language, on a very material point, upon the same footing with the Greek: the objection is, that we neither know, nor can possibly know, like him, the proper use and application of either the Greek or the Latin accents. On these various accounts I am persuaded that the best thing to be done, is to apply, as we now do, our own tones, inflections, and modulations, to both the ancient languages, but with one very material difference from our present practice, that of preserving the true quantity and metre: those tones and inflections are, from our earliest youth, connected with all our associations, emotions, and expressions: they would be lost in the

---

^y These words are in a letter written by Annibal Caracci to his cousin Ludovico, immediately after viewing, for the first time, the works of Coreggio at Parma. The exquisite and highly seducing beauties of that picture, particularly its colouring and pencilling, drew from him this harsh censure of Raphael's Santa Cecilia, and of the dignified figure of Saint Paul.

endeavour to acquire a new set under the name of ancient accent; and such substitutes as we should be able to procure would ill compensate their loss. Each nation, as it seems to me, should make use of its own tones and inflections; for those of other nations, though they might be more harmonious to the ear, would be less congenial. The sum of all is, that the moderns, instead of making any vain endeavours to recover what is irrecoverably lost—ancient accent, tones, &c. should at once restore, what has never been lost, but only partially neglected and perverted—the true quantity and metre. Many persons, I know, have a hankering after ancient accent, and, without much examination of the means, fancy it might be recovered: what then are our principal means for so important a work? the accentual marks, of which the value and authority have lately been very much called in question by a critic of high eminence, and one who had particularly turned his mind towards such points. Their signification too does not seem very exactly agreed upon: we may indeed be pretty sure that the voice was raised on the acute, and lowered again on the grave, or on the unacuted syllables; and if Pericles and Demosthenes, when addressing an Athenian audience, did little more in respect to accent, we certainly may do as much; but if those marks, admitting them to be genuine, and the circumflex, to us a very puzzling one, were the mere skeletons of accentuation; if the charm and effect of Greek accent depended (as it must, more or less, in all languages) on the indescribable variety of tones, inflections,

P

and modulations of the voice, and on the artful transitions, as in music, from low to high, from high to low; if the *anatomy*, as by skilful painters, was covered and adorned with all that was most graceful and becoming; if this highly studied combination, which alone deserves the name, and can alone suggest any adequate notion of Grecian accent, was unattainable by foreigners, though they had the incalculable advantage of hearing the living language spoken in its highest perfection;—what are we likely to attain? In honest truth, we might as well expect, by means of acute, grave, and circumflex, to restore to life the decayed bodies of the ancient Greeks, as to restore, by such means, any resemblance of the effect and charm of their tones and modulations; of all that constituted accent; of all that, no less than their bodies, has irrecoverably perished. What indeed can be expected from the dead letter of the accentual marks, deprived of the vivifying principle—the living speech? nothing but what is of the same character: and the varied tones of an Alcibiades, which enchanted every ear, would bear the same sort of relation to any tones that with such agents we can produce, that the varied and graceful motions of a living Vestris would bear to those of his dead corpse acted upon by Galvanic tractors, an arm or a leg stiffly raised up, and again let down with the same stiff unvaried motion.

PROSE.

———

ALL that has hitherto been said relates to verse only; and it may very naturally be asked, and by the most candid persons, " admitting that a reform is required in verse, what is to be done in prose? is the reform to extend to that also? or are we to have two distinct quantities, one for Homer and Virgil, another for Demosthenes and Cicero? I must own, that if the alternative were unavoidable, it might be as well, if not better, to remain as we are: but I believe there is no danger in the case; for if we once got a settled habit of pronouncing in poetry ἄνᾱξ, ᾰmāns, βρ̆έμ̆ετᾱι, trĕpŭdōs, ᾰιγῐάλῳ, cōnstῑtĕrῐnt, we could never endure the glaring false quantities, the meagre sounds, the hurried and indistinct articulations of ἄνᾰξ, βρ̆έμ̆ετᾰι, cŏnstῑtĕrῐnt, &c. in prose. The reform, should it ever take place, would naturally begin in poetry; it is there more immediately and obviously required, and also, the metre and rhythm being such constant and efficient guides, more easily accomplished; but it must unavoidably at the same moment be gradually going on in prose; at first perhaps in separate words, then in the rhythm of particular passages, and by degrees in the general rhythm and cadence. Whatever difficulties there might be in practice, whatever partial objections might occur, one single advantage, arising from the true quantity, would, in my mind, overbalance them all, that of having the long finals restored throughout the two ancient languages; an advantage only less in prose than in verse. I have fully shewn the extent of it in Greek and Latin verse, and have endeavoured to impress it more sensibly on the minds of my readers, by the opposite method of pointing out the extent of the injury, if we were to shorten every final in English and Italian poetry. It may be said, however, and very truly, that in all such cases habit alone would make any change in the accent appear ridiculous; but (it may be said in answer) in this case the principle upon which the injury is founded, the destruction of variety, is independent of habit. What the effect of shortening every long final must necessarily be, is on reflection obvious to the understanding without the help of examples; as likewise that it must be the same in substance, if not in degree, whether it be done in verse or in prose; examples however occur in every page of English and Italian prose writers; and in the Italian the sense is not less injured than the sound. Every attentive reader must, I think, be struck with them; and, if he should, let him next consider, that in a page of the same length, in Greek or Latin prose, there would be three times as many long finals, every one of which he uniformly *does* shorten; and then let him judge whether, at all events, and in the spite of any drawbacks, the restoration of their due length must not be a most essential improvement.

Our wish to restore this, and a variety of other advantages arising from the same source, would be very much increased, if it can be shewn, that passages which we have been used to admire in oratory would be hardly less strikingly improved by the right quantity than those which I have produced in poetry; and the improvement would not alone be felt in the more artificial arrangement and studied rhythm of oratorical diction: many familiar phrases, where there is any thing of passion or eagerness, would gain an expression in the rhythm which we are now only sensible of from the meaning of the words: on such occasions too, in the eagerness of utterance, a vowel before another might often have been elided in Latin, as it so frequently was in Greek prose: the following instance may be given from the first Olynthiac. I shall in this and in the other passages I may quote place the mark of the ictus, though not *metricus*, under those syllables upon which, according to my judgment, the chief stress might best be laid; in this instance it will accord with our usual pronunciation, as, by means of the elisions, we pronounce the iambi (as in " αυταρ επειτ' αυτοισι) according to quantity; and almost all the rest equally so, there being only one long final, ειτ' ουκ αισχυνεσθε ει μηδ' α παθοιτ' αν, ει δυναιτ' εκεινος, ταυτα ποιησαι καιρον εχοντες ου τολμησετε. In verse the omission of the elided syllables in recitation is absolutely required (and, as we have seen, not in the ancient languages only) both for metre and rhythm; in prose, for rhythm only; but, as we may judge from the passage just quoted, for *that* very strongly; the rapidity and vehemence of that passage would evidently be checked, and in no slight degree, by the restoration of the elided syllables; as, ειτα αισχυνεσθε, ει μηδε ἁ παθοιτε αν, ει δυναιτο εκεινος, and the repeated terminations in ε and ο would tire the ear. What the elisions must have been in Latin verse we know from their structure; what they may have been in Latin prose we have, as far as I am aware, no indication; but it is highly probable, that many passages in Cicero owed their brevity, rapidity, and energy, to such elisions as those in Demosthenes. It appears that the Romans, in familiar discourse, and in comedy, which comes nearest to it, almost suppressed the first vowel on such iambi as *bonum, malum,* &c. and for the obvious purpose of making them still more *celeres;* and pronounced them *b'num, m'lum,* as the French from *petit* make *p'tit:* when so pronounced, and likewise with an elision, nothing can go on more vehemently than the sort of Latin curse, " abi'n m'lam rem ;" nothing more languidly than " ā'bĭ ĭn mā'lăm rē'm:" one might indeed suppose from the cadence, that a lover was bidding farewell to his mistress, and tenderly saying, " go, and good luck betide thee." Compare again the two modes in Cæsar's well-known speech to the master of the vessel in a storm: " quid times? Caesarem vehis:" in our mode, " quĭd tīmĕs? Caēsărĕm vēhĭs; as likewise his brief command at Pharsalia: " miles! feri faciem." The spondee, "miles," is the word of attention; the iambus and anapæst, " feri faciem," rapidly and energetically convey the order; an order which, perhaps,

decided the fate of the battle and of the world. Lay
the accent on all the first syllables, and see whether
there will be the same energy and rapidity in the three
false quantities: " mĭ′lĕs! fē′rĭ fă′cĭĕm [z]." I will give
one other instance of a very different kind, but not less
familiar to every reader: " Paete non dolet;" we say,
" Pae′tĕ nŏn dō′lĕt :" there is a good deal of difference
in so short a sentence, on the mere score of variety in
the cadence between a trochee at the beginning, with a
pyrrhic at the end, and a trochee in each place; but
the essential difference is in the ictus and emphasis on
non, instead of its being, in every way false, upon *dōlet*.

It is time to give an oratorical example of some
length, and for the express purpose of contrasting the
two modes: I will first, however, as a sort of inter-
mediate step between the regular well-known metres
and dignified prose, try a passage in Pindar, where the
force and richness of the expressions perfectly accord

[z] We depend most on the last syllable for distinct articulation and
effect: to give a familiar instance, a gamekeeper calling his pointers by
their names, says, like any scholar, Jū nŏ, Plū′tŏ, Dĭ′dŏ; but if one of
them misbehaves, he claps an accent on the last syllable, and cries out,
Dĭdō′, confound you, what are you about there? The sound of monosyllables, however loudly you may try to utter them, is dead; you want another
syllable, in order to lay a strong accent on one of them: and this, without
such reflections, is felt by the unlearned. A gamekeeper of mine (to go on
with the same dramatis personæ) wanted Juno to come to him; and after
screaming several times to no purpose, *here here*, he divided the word into
two syllables, and with an accent on the first cried out Hē′rĕ Hē′rĕ.
" Your gamekeeper," said a friend of mine who was with us, " is calling
Juno by her Greek name." If a reform had then been made, H′ǫń would
not so well have suited my friend's allusion.

with the grandeur of the sentiments: and I think it
will appear, that by pronouncing it according to quantity, the rhythm would be much better suited to both.
I must remind the reader, that the advantages I have
ascribed to such a mode are, fulness of sound, distinctness of articulation, diversity in the cadence and the
terminations of the words themselves, a varied and
harmonious connection of them with one another, and a
general flow of harmony resulting from that connection:
I shall make two transcripts of the passage, marking in
the first the right quantities, and also some of the
places where, in consequence of observing them, the
words appear to blend happily together. In the second
I shall place the long mark on the syllables upon which
we lay the accent, and the short mark on those upon
which we do *not* lay it. I will only request the reader
to suspend his judgment (which, in the most candid,
must in some degree be biassed by habit) till he has
acquired, as he soon may, the new habit; so as to read
fluently according to quantity, to give the full length
to all the long syllables, and the full expression to
every part:

'Ο μεγας δε κινδυ-

νος αναλκιν ου φω-

τα λαμβανει. θανειν δ' οἱσιν αναγκα,

τι κε τις ανωνυμον γηρας εν σκοτῳ

καθημενος ἑψοι ματαν, ἁπαντων

καλων αμμορος· αλλ' εμοι μεν ουτοσι

αθλος γ' ὑποκεισεται· τυ δε
πραξιν φιλαν διδοι.

ὅ μἔγᾱς δἔ κῑνδῡ-
νὅς ἄνᾱλκῐν οὐ φῶ-
τᾱ λᾱμβᾰνεῖ. θᾰνεῖν δ' ὅἰσῐν ἄνᾱγκᾰ,
τῐ κἔ τῐς ἄνὡνῡμὅν γῆρᾱς ἔν σκὅτῷ
κᾰθῆμἔνὅς 'ἔψοῐ μᾱτᾰν, 'ᾰπᾱντῶν
κᾰλῶν ᾰμμὅρὅς. ἄλλ' ἔμὅι μἔν ὁῦτὅσῐ
ᾱθλὅς γ' ὑπὅκεῖσἔτᾱι. τῦ δἔ
πρᾱξῐν φῐλᾰν δῐδοῐ.

In the first transcript the opening sentence termi-
nates upon a long final, and thence has that firmness of
rhythm which suits the expression. The second sentence has seven long finals, and only four short ones,
which, however, give sufficient variety, without weaken-
ing the energy. In the third short sentence, every final
is long, but the want of variety is, in my mind, amply
compensated; for it seems to me that these continued
long finals very strikingly express the deliberate firmness
of resolve. The fourth and last, containing a short
prayer to Neptune, finely concludes this noble passage;
and the rhythm, formed by a pyrrhic, followed by a
spondee, and that by two iambi, has a varied and harmonious cadence worthy of all the rest. How far the
comment I have ventured to make is well founded, the
reader will judge; but I feel very confident that he will
think the whole very materially improved by the right
quantities, when he compares the first transcript with

the second: in *that*, every final is of course made short; the unavoidable consequence of which (not to mention the numerous and glaring false quantities) is monotony and disconnection: these prevail in every part; but the perfection of them and of flatness is in the concluding sentence, τῦ δὲ πρᾶξῖν φῖλᾶν δῖδοῖ. If this prayer had been addressed to the deity with the quantities so perverted, and such a rhythm in consequence, Neptune, though not much connected with the Muses, would certainly have laid his σκηπανιον on the suppliant, and not quite in so gentle and friendly a manner as he did on the Ajaces. What then in such a case would Apollo have done? If in a playful mood, he would have treated him like Midas; if in a severe one, like Marsyas.

I will now try the same experiment in prose, and shall likewise give the example in the Greek language, as being in itself more full and sonorous, and also because two of the long vowels are marked to the eye. The example is taken from Demosthenes; and the passage has been so often quoted, as to be in every person's memory, and perhaps on that account more unfavourable to my purpose than one less familiar; as the habitual manner of pronouncing it must more strongly excite a prejudice against any proposed alteration. Η βουλεσθε ειπε μοι περιιοντες αυτων πυνθανεσθαι κατα την αγοραν, λεγεται τι καινον; γενοιτο γαρ αν τι καινοτερον, η Μακεδων ανηρ Αθηναιους καταπολεμων, και τα των Ελληνων διοικων. I will first observe, generally, that in this passage, the difference between laying the stress, on the one hand, upon all the diphthongs, and on all the long, full, and

sonorous vowels, or, on the other hand, upon some of
them only, and often on the short meagre vowels, is no
less striking than in the line formerly quoted from
Homer: there we have, with our accents,

Αἰγιἄλῷ μἔγἄλἄ βρἔμἔταἴ,

and here we have ἄγὄρἄν, λἔγἔταἴ, κἄινὄτἔρὄν, Μἄκἔδὦν,
ἄνήρ, Ἀθήναιοῦς, κἄτἄπὄλἔμὦν, Ἑλλήνὦν, δἴοἴκὦν.
Another circumstance of no slight consequence in
prose, though of still greater in verse, is, that when the
long finals are universally shortened, that continued
connected chain, on which cadence and harmony so
much depend, is perpetually broken: every word, therefore, which ends on a long syllable, should have the
length of that syllable sufficiently marked, or the conti-
nuity will be dissolved: thus if we say πὔνθἄνἔσθαἴ, κατα
will stand alone; and we can hardly help making it a
trochee instead of a pyrrhic, especially as we accent
ἄ'γὄρἄν on the first syllable, detaching it from την; and
again, by a similar accent, λἔ'γἔταἴ from every thing.
On the other hand, when θαι and ραν are both accented,
the rhythm goes on with a continued and well connected
rapidity, in anapæsts, or on a choriambus and anapæsts,
θαι κατα την αγοραν λεγεται: after which, τι καινον expressively closes the sentence at the note of interrogation,
the spondee giving time to dwell sarcastically on the
great object of idle enquiry. The next sentence begins
with the same sort of vehement and well blended rhythm,
γενοιτο γαρ αν τι καινοτερον, which in our mode of accenting is, γἔνοἴτὄ γάρ ἄν τι κἄἴνὄτἔρὄν. I am sure, at least,

that it is thus that we lay the accent in the last word,
and most unluckily, as (independently of the false quantity) from the accent being on the omicron instead of
the diphthong, the sound, and what is worse, the sense
of the word is injured : the sense and expression of
καινον in the positive, even when by position it is a
spondee, are much more marked by the first than the
last syllable; and therefore, in the *comparative* καῐνό-
τἔρὄν, the same length, the same stress should be given
to the same syllable, or the sort of echo, which recals
and enforces the expression, will completely be lost.
The concluding words of the passage exemplify all that
has been advanced, at least as strongly as the preceding
part : when we say, Μἄ'κἔδῶν ἄ'νῆρ Ᾱ'θῆνᾱΐοῦς κἄ'τᾰπŏ'λἔμῶν,
we lay the stress, as in former cases, on many of the
short vowels, and omit laying it on any of the long ones
in the finals, and of course deprive the words of the
true fulness of their sound, and keep them separate and
distinct, instead of blending them with one another,
and, in my mind, do no less injury to their characteristic expression.   In this concluding sentence, the long
established power and authority of the Athenians are to
be placed in opposition to the newly acquired influence
and successful encroachments of Philip; and after the
contemptuous though rapid and sonorous words, Μακεδων ανηρ, no word could have been more happily invented, for the purpose of being dwelt upon and impressed upon the ears of such an audience, as Αθηναιους,
the last long syllable of which makes the four short
ones of κᾰτᾰπŏλἔμῶν glide on smoothly, till the voice

rests upon μων. Lastly, having thus placed Philip in opposition to the Athenians, and the disgrace of being vanquished by him, in contrast with their ancient glory, Demosthenes winds up the whole by the same sort of opposition between the man of Macedon and the collective body of the Greeks, when the word Ἑλληνων, of three long syllables, is no less suited to the expression than Aθηναιους. By making it Ἑλλήνων, we not only destroy the quantity and the expression, but, what must have been of great consequence before such an audience, we spoil the finishing cadence of so marked a period. Demosthenes, I should conceive, was very unlikely to end it with two trisyllables of exactly the same cadence, as Ἑλλήνων and διοἶκων, and the Athenians as unlikely to endure such an ending: but by giving the true quantity to Ἑλληνων, you get rid of the uniform jingle; and fulness of tone, variety, harmony, and expression, are at once restored, where they are most peculiarly required.

ON A NEW MODE, OF PRONOUNCING THE ANCIENT LANGUAGES.

IN a former part of this Essay I have slightly mentioned a mode of pronouncing the iambus and the pyrrhic, originally, I believe, introduced at the Charter House, which has of late years very much prevailed. The old mode (according to which I have hitherto marked those feet above the line) is to place the accent immediately after the vowel, as με′γα and ma′gis, equally so whether they were iambi or pyrrhics : the new mode, to place it after the consonant, as μεγ′α and mag′is, to pronounce them as we should if written μεγγ′α and magg′is, in which way I shall write them in this particular discussion. The ground of this alteration is, that με′γα and ma′gis are positive trochees, that the first syllable is evidently long, and that it ought to be made short in pronunciation ; than which nothing can be more just ; the question, however, is, whether the alteration be an effectual remedy, or indeed any remedy at all. I trust it has been satisfactorily shewn in the early part of these pages, that our accent uniformly gives length to the accented syllable, the unaccented being uniformly

short ; consequently that all dissyllables accented on the
first must be trochees ; when after the vowel perfect,
when after the consonant imperfect, but still trochees. I
have also shewn, what indeed is most evident, that we
have a number of iambi in English perfect standards for
the quantity and cadence of that foot in Latin, though
we never make use of them for that purpose, pronouncing the Latin word ā′go, not like our English word ăgō′,
and this universally throughout that language. In the
Greek we give to some dissyllables (contracted by elision from trisyllables) what I consider as the true quantity and cadence of the iambus, as γυναιχ᾽, επειτ᾽, accenting them on the final ; are they considered in the same
light by the advocates of this system ? If the answer be
in the affirmative, then they are acknowledged standards
for the pronunciation of that foot, and there can be
only one standard; yet in the same line, a word equally
an iambus from the structure of the verse, is pronounced in the new way βελλος : both cannot be right ;
and therefore they should consistently either change their
pronunciation of the first to αυταρ εππ῾ειτ᾽ αυτοισι, or that
of the second to β̄ελ̄ος εχεπευχες εφιεις. There can scarcely
be a doubt that this last mode should be adopted
in this and in al' cases, as invariably agreeing in
metre and rhythm with the few but exact standards in
Greek, and the numerous undeniable standards in English, and as being in all cases consistent. Why then, it
may be asked, when so simple, obvious, and consistent,
a mode presented itself, was recourse had to a mode
which already appears (and will appear more strongly)

to be inconsistent with our occasional pronunciation of the iambus in Greek, and our constant pronunciation of it in English? Two causes may be assigned, closely connected with each other: the one, that there is no dissyllable in English really a pyrrhic, which in that case *would* have been, as so many iambi *are*, standards for pronunciation: the other, that a number of them are falsely considered as such, and as perfect standards for the quantity and sound of that foot in Greek and in Latin: on this very material point I shall offer some observations, in addition to those I have already made. All such words as *bod'y, berr'y, mon'ey*, &c. the accent being after the consonant, are, as I have ventured to assert, falsely considered as pyrrhics, and standards; their first syllable being supposed to be positively, not comparatively, short: such words, when a preceding syllable is added to them, often form a dactyl, as *some-body, nobody, strawberry*, &c. and it is evident that the two last syllables of a dactyl must be a pyrrhic; and no less so, that in all distinct dactyls we uniformly pronounce them as such, whether in ancient or in modern languages: on these grounds the two last syllables of *somebody, strawberry*, &c. must be pyrrhics, must have the true sound and cadence of that foot, and be standards for its pronunciation. What is that sound? not that of *bod'y* or *berr'y*, but, as every one will perceive who first sounds the dactyls, and then the two last syllables as he did sound them, *bŏdў̆, bĕrrў̆*, just like *cŏlŏr* without the *dis*. *Discólor* is at once felt to be no dactyl; why? because our accent is on the second sylla-

ble ; change it to the first, *díscolor*, the dactyl is restored : in the same manner *somebod'y* is no dactyl, but
an amphibrach ; shift the accent, and the dactyl *sómebody* is restored. What is then the process by which
the imperfect trochees *bod'y*, *berr'y*, &c. become pyrrhics ? clearly by the accent being taken from them,
which made their first syllable long, and by its being
laid on the first of the compound *sómebody*, *stráwberry* ;
and our ancestors, when they formed those compounds,
seem, by a sort of instinct, to have *felt*, though they
might not *know*, that accent gave length : and thus to
have reversed what Madame du Deffand so ingeniously
says of the Duchess of Choiseul, " Elle sait qu'elle
m'aime, mais ne le sent pas." It may perhaps be said
by the advocates for English pyrrhics : admitting that
these dissyllables must be deprived of their accent before they can, as pyrrhics, form the ends of dactyls, still
they are the only examples you have produced of such
a conversion ; can you give any of real acknowledged
trochees so converted ? In answer to the question,
which is a very fair one, I shall propose the following
examples, in all the different vowels, *Mary*, *rosemary* ;
keeper, *gamekeeper* ; *finite*, *infinite* ; *holder*, *Stadt-
holder* ; *jury*, *perjury*. There is at least one instance
of an *iambus* being converted by the same process, as
from *belów*, *fúrbelow* : restore the accent to the iambus,
keeping that on the first syllable, the dactyl becomes an
amphimacer, the pyrrhic an iambus, *fúrbelów*. It is
thus used in an old catch for the sake of the rhythm,
and of the waggery,

Adam cātch'd Eve by the fúrbelów,
And that's the oldest catch I know.

I have mentioned the want of any dissyllabic standard for the pyrrhic as a principal cause of the false pronunciation of the iambus; yet it seems strange, that
because we have no standard for the one, we should
therefore make no use of the numerous and perfect
standards for the other : the fact is, that there was a
real difficulty and embarrassment respecting the new-
fangled pyrrhic, as connected with the new-fangled iambus; thus, for instance, when in our usual method we
pronounce the iambus *mărī*, and the pyrrhic *mărĕ*, as
trochees, both, though equally false quantities, keep
each other in countenance; and so in the new
way, though likewise false quantities, do *marr'i*
and *marr'e:* but if any one were to pronounce the iambus with an accent on the last syllable, as it evidently ought to be pronounced, and the pyrrhic with it
on the first, there could be no doubt that one of them
must be wrong, and as little which of them ; especially
if both the words occurred on the same line ; as in

Nam Venus orta mari tutum mare praestat eunti.

Who, after hearing the first syllable of *mari* so decidedly short, so exactly of the same cadence with *deny,*
rely, could endure *marr'i* as an iambus? whoever could,
might very well endure *denn'y* and *rell'y* in English.
Had there been any English dissyllables possessing as
decidedly and convincingly the quantity, cadence, and
true character of the pyrrhic as those I have mentioned

present of the iambus, perhaps in regard to those two feet at least the rule might have been dispensed with; and possibly, from the manifest advantage of such a change in a part of the system, similar changes might have been made in other parts, till the whole of it was abandoned. One glaring vice of this new mode is its inconsistency; for, admitting that by placing the accent after the consonant, *magg'is* became a true pyrrhic, and both its syllables equally short, what happens when in the same verse it is first a pyrrhic and then an iambus? as in

Et magis atque magis.

I understand that in both places they are pronounced exactly alike; and on this ground I would ask (not caring what the answer might be), is *gis* long or short? if long, there can be no pyrrhic; if short, no iambus; and it cannot be both long and short. Again, admitting what is obviously inadmissible, that by changing *mágis* into *magg'is*, a true pyrrhic, and likewise a true iambus, are acquired, what is to be done where the vowel is followed by another, as in *meus?* there is no remedy, unless the rule be given up, which can never be expected from an advocate for the old system, as well as for the new mode; they therefore are reduced to the mortifying disgrace of pronouncing *méus*, *túus*, &c. like the common herd, and to make them, knowingly, positive trochees. This, though mortifying, was unavoidable; but where a *u* is followed by a consonant, as in πυρι, *furor*, &c. the new mode might be, according to their own principles, and ought to have been made use of;

they, however, have chosen to retain the old pronunciation, and their practice is clearly at variance with their
principle. The principle is, that the vowel is to be
passed over in pyrrhics and iambi wherever this can be
done ; it cannot in κυων, but may, and ought consistently, to be done in κυνε, the first syllable of which
would then be pronounced like the first of *cunn'ing* ;
that of *con'ey* (a striking specimen of the difference between our spelling and our speaking) has the same
sound, and the whole word—with as good a claim to be
a pyrrhic as any other trochee—exactly that of κυν'ε or
κυνν'ε. Why then against the principle and the general
practice in consequence of it is the old pronunciation
retained ? I know not ; having merely heard the fact
from a person bred at the Charter House, but no cause
was assigned. It may perhaps have been observed, that
in κύν'ε the sound of the *u* as *we* sound the vowel is preserved ; whereas in κυν'ε or κυνν'ε, as in *cunn'ing* or
pun'ish, it is lost, and in lieu of it something very like the
French *e muet* is substituted; for *que ni* would indicate
to a Frenchman the sound of *coney* as nearly as the
different accents and habits of the two languages would
admit of ; and is, indeed, the way in which he would
pronounce the word. This change of the sound is certainly a very mischievous consequence of the change in
the placing of the accent ; and he who first introduced
it may, in this case, have retained the old pronunciation
of κύν ε, though so positive a trochee, " majoris fugiens
opprobria culpae." But although in respect to the *u*,
the greater sin, or at least one of two sins, be avoided,

it is not in other vowels : I imagine that the first syllable of κορρ'υν has, in the new mode, the sound of *for* or
of *cor* in Latin ; if so, then the true sound of the *o* is as
completely gone as that of the *u* in κυνν'ε. The first of
κορρ'υν and of *morrow* are alike ; not an *o*, but a short
au: lengthen *morr'ow*, you have *mau'ro;* shorten *mau'-
ro*, you have *morrow ;* in the same manner lengthen
κορρ'υν, you have, in English characters, *caur-yoon ;*
shorten it, and you return to κορρ'υν. The sounds of the
a and the *e* are likewise often changed by the new
mode, though less offensively. Another consequence of
passing over the *u* to the consonant may have had some
little influence ; that of its often producing a ludicrous
similarity to English words, as in the one just mentioned of *coney; sup'er* becomes *supp'er ; Cur'ius,
curr'y us,* &c. This however would scarcely be worth
thinking of, if it did not add to a number of others also
derived from the new mode : *de'cus, Ma'rius, da'mus,*
are changed to *deck us, marry us, damn us;* and στίχη,
φίλη, *si'le,* to *sticky, filly, silly.* Again, βέλη becomes
belly, γάμον *gammon, pàti patty, céler cellar :* and there
is a very appropriate epithet to a gay damsel at a
supper mentioned by Horace, " Damalis merr'i." Swift,
in his ludicrous etymologies, has supposed the name of
Hector's wife to have been given to her from that of her
father, Andrew Mackay, a well-known Scotch pedlar ;
the old pronunciation did not at all suit it; the new
one as exactly as Swift could have wished ; and, with
this surname of Μαχχ'η, furnishes a crowd of Christian
names; *dóle,* φάνη, *sále, gére,* τόμη, *róger,* δίκη, are at

once changed to Dolly, Fanny, Sally, Jerry, Tommy, Roger, and Dicky. This last familiar diminutive ill accords with the august person of Justice;

ἡ συνοικος των κατω θεων Δικη.

In this line our trochaic propensity is peculiarly unlucky: three successive trochees at the end of an iambic, and such trochees!

One of the first things that strikes us in the change from the old pronunciation of the pyrrhic and iambus, is the ambiguities it gives rise to: *érat* becomes *errat;* as in

Hoc errat in votis; moddus agri non itta magnus,

and,

Non formosus err'at, sed err'at facundus Ulysses.

Těrěs, an epithet applied to beauty, even to the neck of Venus, is changed to *terr'es.* Penelope, in Ovid's Epistle, is afraid lest Ulysses at his return should think her changed from a girl, not (as we are now taught to pronounce the word) into an old woman, but into a year:

Facta videbor ann'us:

and Horace tells Lyce that she is growing into one:

Fis ann'us et tamm'en [a].

---

[a] An old Housekeeper at Kensington Palace used to make a metamorphosis of a similar kind: on shewing a picture of Perseus and Andromeda, she always said, "Ladies and Gentlemen, there is Anno Domini chained to the Rock."

These ambiguities, it will be said, have been guarded against: *érat* and *ánus*, as every body once called them, are by the new mode to have the sound we used to give to *err'at* and *ann'us;* but we are taught by the same mode to pronounce the *real* trochees as the Italians do, *er'rat* and *an'nus*, carefully separating each consonant. This certainly does form a distinction; it is one, however, that requires great attention to the sounds, both in the speaker and the hearer, and which would be quite unnecessary, were the evidently true sound given to the iambus, and the no less certainly true one to the pyrrhic, as being founded on our own pronunciation of that foot, though somewhat in disguise. The Italian mode of pronouncing *er'rat, an'nus*, &c. I could wish to be universally adopted; and we should have a real obligation to the Charter House for having introduced and practised that mode[b], were it not connected with the unjustifiable one of *err'at* and *ann'us;* the strongest objection to which is, that it does not in the smallest degree answer the proposed object. This will at once be seen, and in the most striking manner, by means of a line already quoted: in the old mode,

Νοῦσον ἄνὰ στρᾱ'τὸν ὤ'ρσὲ κᾰ'κῆν,

---

[b] Another part of the Charter House mode of pronouncing ought by no means to be omitted: it is, that when a long vowel precedes a single consonant, as *é-ruet, ó-mine*, &c. they dwell on the vowel instead of passing over it to the consonant, as is generally done, as *er'uet, om'ine*. This is a most decided improvement, and one that, together with the detached Italian utterance of *er-rat, an-nus*, &c. will I hope be universally adopted.

is the flattest prose: is it less so when in the new mode we say,

Νōύσὸν ᾱνν'α στρᾱττ'ὸν ω̄'ρσᾰ κᾱκκ'ῆν.

Is it not evident, that no slight degree of harshness and cacophony is added, while the false quantities and the trochaic cadence are preserved? and equally evident, that by restoring the genuine sound and cadence of the pyrrhic and the iambi, those of the verse altogether are as fine as in any verse in the poem:

Νουσον ανα στρατον ωρσε κακην, ολεκοντο δε λαοι.

Were no other verse quoted, nothing more said on the subject, this single example would, in my opinion, be a clear condemnation both of the general system and of the partial change; I shall, however, produce other quotations of various kinds, all tending to shew, that the metre and rhythm are no less spoiled by the new than by the old mode, and the sound much more. In the following line, every thing quite to the end is disfigured:

Ρε̄χθε̄'ντὸς κᾱκκ'οῠ ε̆στ' ᾱκκ'ο̄ς εῡρειν· ᾱλ'λᾱ πο̄λλ'υ πρῑν.

In the beginning of the line I am going to quote, a most ludicrous jingle is made by the new mode, followed by an uncouth word; neither of which appeared in the old mode:

Ᾱλ'λᾱ μᾱλλ'ᾱ στῑχχ'ᾱς ε̄ιμῐ̈ δῐ̈ᾱ'μπε̆ρε̆ς:

I have in a former part given various instances of the extreme injury done to rapidity by the old mode of pronouncing the iambus followed by the pyrrhic: is less injury done to it by the new one in παρρ'ος κονν'ιν, μαλλ'α σχεδδ'ον, χαμμ'αι θορρ'ε? or by

Īl'lĕ vōll'ăt, sīmm'ŭl ār'vă fū'gă, sīmm'ŭl aē'quŏră vē'rrens?

But admitting that voll'at, simm'ul, &c. are all that their warmest advocates suppose them to be, the change would be hardly worth making, unless it were complete: in the midst of them we here see the avowed trochee, fu'ga; and in the verse I am going to quote there is an iambus and two pyrrhics of that kind:

Hĕu fū'gĕ nā'tĕ dē'ă tē'quĕ hĭs ā'ĭt ē'ripĕ flāmmis[b].

[b] In all the verses hitherto quoted, the pyrrhic, I believe, ought to be joined to the preceding long syllable, and to form the end of a dactyl, as "Hēu fŭgĕ, hĭs ăĭt:" but in the next verse,

Hostis habet muros; ruit alto a culmine Troja,

the sense requires that it should be joined to the subsequent long syllable, ruit alt', and form in pronunciation an anapæst: it is still more strongly required in

cur hoc?
Dicam si potero, male ver'm examinat omnis.

"Dicam si potero male" would be a ridiculous contresens. It sometimes happens that a pyrrhic should be pronounced distinctly by itself, as

Rettuleris pannum;—refer—et sine vivat ineptus:

There is a line (already mentioned for a different purpose) in the animated description of the Phalanx, where the iambus followed by the pyrrhic, when both are rightly pronounced, gives a striking dactylic impetus to the rhythm ;

Ασπις αρ' ασπιδ' ερειδε, κορυς κορυν, ανερα δ' ανηρ [d].

On the other hand, in our usual way, the verse, after a triumphant beginning, falters, and almost stops in the middle, where it should firmly and rapidly advance ;

Ā'σπῐ̄ς ᾰρ' ᾱ'σπῐ̄δ' ε̄ρε̄ῑδε̄,-κο̄'ρῠ̆ς κο̄'ρῠ̆ν,-ᾱ'νε̄ρᾰ̆ δ' ᾱ'νηρ.

In the new mode, to parody a distich in Churchill's Rosciad ;

When the swift Dactyl's in its full career,
How vilely κορρ'υς κορρ'υν grates the ear !

I shall next give an example of the same two feet employed in the same part of the verse, but with a very different sort of expression ; it is from Virgil's third

---

but the strongest instance is in Anna's speech, when she sees Dido expiring :

Extinxti me teque soror, populumque, patresque
Sidonios, urbemque tuam : dătĕ, vulnera lymphis
Abluam.

The sense is, " Date lymphas, ut illis abluam vulnera," but the omission strikingly expresses hurry and agitation : it is obvious that we could neither say " tuam date," nor " date vulnera."

d Iliad xiii. 131.

Eclogue. I shall put down the preceding line, partly for the sake of connection, but more for that of shewing how quickly and lightly the rhythm goes off, when the elided syllables are omitted; how heavily it drags, when they are distinctly pronounced, and the quantity disregarded. I shall first give the lines as in all probability they were, then as, in the new mode, they *are*, pronounced:

> Phyllid' am' ant' alias, nam me decedere flevit,
> Et longum formose vale, vale, inquit, Iola.

> Phyll'ĭdă āmm'ŏ ā'ntĕ āll'ĭás, năm mē' dĕcē'dĕrĕ flĕ'vit,
> Ĕt lō'ngŭm fŏrmō'sĕ vāll'ĕ, vāll'ĕ, ĭ'nquĭt, Ĭō'la.

Metre absolutely requires, and rhythm in a great degree, that the two syllables of every spondee should be long, and equally long, no less in recitation than in structure; but to make such a spondee as *lōngūm* a trochee, is at once to sin against metre, rhythm, and expression: instead of shortening the syllable, we ought, as guided by the ictus, not only to give it length, but stress: this, however, though I did not like to pass over it, is not to my present purpose: the iambus and pyrrhic are, and very strikingly. When the last syllable of the iambus has its due length and stress, and is uttered in rather a full and high tone, and when we appear to linger on it, and then connect and blend it with the pyrrhic nearly as one word—vale-vale—the last farewell, being breathed out in a weaker and lower tone, seems a faint echo of the first; and, in my mind, is very happily suited to the expression. I cannot perceive in what way the pronunciation of vale, vale, could be altered, so as to be more exactly suited to the quantity, cadence, and genuine character of the two feet, whether single or joined together; va'le, va'le, are avowedly trochees, and perfect; val'e, val'e, are also, though not avowedly, trochees, but imperfect : both, therefore, are equally at variance with the metre and the rhythm. We had always been taught to lay the accent after the vowel; we are now taught to lay it after the consonant : in either way, the sound being the very same, there can be no sort of distinction between the two feet ! can this ever be right, between any two feet ? The cadence too, in the new mode, is that which had uniformly been given to *vall'e,*

Hic in reducta valle Caniculae.

The trochee, as we pronounce it, has a short accent ; but we do not (a distinction which should never be lost sight of) make a *false,* but an *imperfect* quantity: now if it be true that the first syllable of *val'e* or *vall'e* (for the sound is the same) is really short, and that such a passing over of the vowel is the proper method of giving shortness, we ought consistently to say *cann'icull'ae,* a ditrochee, answering precisely to *vall'e vall'e ;* while *cani'culae,* no less precisely, answers to *vale-vale.*

There is a line in the sixth Eclogue, where the idea of an echo, the iambus and pyrrhic being in the same position, is more immediately and forcibly suggested by the subject ;

His adjungít Hylam nautae quo fonte relictum
Clamassent, ut littus Hyla-Hyla omne sonaret.

We may apply to this verse the same sort of comparison
as to the other; " littus Hyla-Hyla" answers to " condis
amabile;" " līttŭs Hȳll'ă Hȳll'ă" to " cōndĭs ămm'ăbĭll'ĕ."

I shall lastly give an example of an hexameter and
pentameter. They are the two concluding lines of an
epigram on a beautiful female musician, from whose
various charms and attractions there was no escaping.
I shall put down the two preceding lines, but in *them*
shall only mark the *right* quantities.

Ποι σε φυγω; παντη με περιστησασιν ερωτες·

Ουδ' ὁσον αμπνευσαι βαιον εωσι χρονον.

Η γαρ μοι μορφη βαλλει ποθον, η παλι μουσα,

Η χαρις, η—τι λεγω; παντα πυρι φλεγομαι.

Many things in these lines will strike the attentive
reader, judging only from the marks, and their evident
effect: first, the variety given to the words themselves,
and to the whole rhythm, by the intermixture of long
and short finals: secondly, the connection that is produced by means of the long ones: thirdly, the perfect
dactyls which are formed by means of the pyrrhics,
when they have their true cadence, and the preceding
syllables their due length. All this will strike him
much more strongly when he compares the last distich
and its marks with the same distich as I shall now
mark it:

Ἦ' γὰρ μοῖ μό'ρφῆ βᾶλ'λεῖ πόθθ'όν, ἤ πᾶλλ'ῑ μόύσα,
Ἤ χᾶρρ'ῑς, ἤ-τῖ λεγγ'ῶ; πᾶ'ντᾶ πῦ'ρῑ φλε'γόμαῖ.

In these two lines, as they are marked, there is not a
vestige of metre or rhythm from beginning to end:
there is neither spondee nor dactyl, unless it be the
reversed anapæst, φλεγόμαῖ, which will hardly be claimed;
and, to my ear, the frequent recurrence of the sound of
a consonant in the first syllable, as ποθθον, παλλι, χαρρις,
λεγγω, is at once both harsh and monotonous, and, to
my judgment, equally destructive both of metre and
rhythm.

We have been in the constant habit of applying
our accent to the ancient languages, just as we use
it in our own, and in so doing have been led into
numberless errors of the grossest kind: accent, however,
is not to blame, but only the mode of applying it:
change the mode, and there cannot be a safer or more
effectual guide. The manner of changing it is the
simplest and easiest possible: instead of laying it on
those syllables, whether long or short, upon which the
Romans laid their's, let it be laid on *every* long syllable,
and never on any short one: the accented syllables
would then, as in English, be long, the unaccented
short. Were we to follow this plain rule, we could
never make a false quantity; it would be highly proper,
however, in addition, to adopt the ancient guide of recitation, the ictus metricus, which would *then* always
act in cooperation with accent, never in opposition to
it; the true sound of the pyrrhic should also be strictly

attended to; and, till our habits were settled, it might be well to use the different marks. This mode, and these marks, would ensure the great essential points in recitation, those of quantity, metre, and of the genuine rhythm; and with them many others, as variety, euphony, connection, and expression, with ease and distinctness of articulation.

CONCLUSION.

—————

THE subject on which I first presented my ideas to the public, is certainly of a very different kind from that upon which I have now ventured to offer them; but it is rather a singular coincidence, that in each I should have made an open and direct attack on a mode and practice established in my own country. In my Essays on the Picturesque, I endeavoured to shew that our English system of laying out grounds, or, as it has lately been called, of *Landscape Gardening*, is at variance with all the principles of landscape painting, and with the practice of all the most eminent masters: in the present publication it has been my endeavour to shew, that our system of pronouncing the ancient languages is equally at variance with the principles and established rules of ancient prosody, and the practice of the best poets; and what makes the coincidence more exact, is, that in speaking of the mischievous consequences of both systems, I have in each laid the greatest stress on the destruction of variety and connection. These two qualities are equally indispensable in the composition and arrangement of scenery, and of versification; and a succession of clumps, unconnected with one another, and with all other objects, has as close an analogy with a succession of trochees uncombined with one another, and with all other feet, as could well take place between things so different in their nature; their want of variety is no less obvious than their want of connection, from which, indeed, it principally arises. I rather flatter myself, that since the publication of the Essays, fewer distinct clumps have been planted, and fewer clumps of trees made as clumplike, as their originally varied character would allow of; how far the present publication may prevent iambi, spondees, and pyrrhics, from being converted into trochees; anapæsts and amphimacers into dactyls, &c. time will shew. No one writes on a controverted or debatable subject, without the hope of making proselytes to his opinions; but, in the present case, supposing the errors and means of correcting them which I have pointed out, to be ever so generally admitted in theory, there would still be a long way from such admission to practice. We all know how natural it is that men of a certain age should be attached to old habits; how unwillingly they give up what they were taught to admire in their younger days: who then could expect them, not only to acknowledge that their present pronunciation of Greek and Latin is founded in error, but to unlearn it, and begin teaching themselves, when they have no longer the same aptitude, a totally new pronunciation of much the greater part of both the ancient languages? I certainly do not; and my hopes of a practical reform, as far as they go, are founded on the rising generation. In youth the habits are less settled, the organs more flexible, and new habits more easily acquired; and should my Essay have the good fortune to attract attention and be generally read, it may not, perhaps, be too much to expect, that in different schools and colleges, some young men of acute and inquiring minds, and looked up to by others, may be struck with what they had never reflected upon; may be induced to try, what they never had thought of trying; and to repeat the experiments of which I have given the result, on verses and passages of their own choosing. Such a practice, without their thinking of it as such, would, at their age, soon enable them to recite with ease and readiness, according to quantity; and the advantages of it in a thousand ways (besides the very essential one of being right instead of wrong) would be so apparent, that many of their schoolfellows or fellow collegiates might be led to do, what it is natural to do in such cases—to imitate what they began to admire, and to ridicule what they began to despise. Those of the same standing with themselves, who still adhered to the old system, would be afraid of repeating before them a Greek or Latin line, as the false quantities, lame metre, &c. &c. no longer current, would instantly be detected, and held up to derision; and this is the natural progress of reformation of every kind. But what would the grave masters of schools and the veteran tutors of colleges do, if they could not stem the torrent; and found that false quantities, even from their mouths, if not openly ridiculed, were laughed at *sous cape?* I hardly know, unless they took lessons from these juvenile Doctors,

And scholars to the youths they taught became.

Ridicule, if founded on evident truth and reason, is irresistible ; and by degrees the whole mass of corruption would be purified. Such is the fond dream of an author, as to the effect of a work, which may produce none of any kind : but I must be allowed to finish my dream. I shall suppose then, that the true quantity, metre, and rhythm, in recitation, were triumphant, and firmly established : that after the lapse of some centuries, when the present system and my book had long been forgotten, a stray copy of this last was discovered, and brought into notice by some collector and reader of such things ; it would then be a very curious record of a system so perversely and mischievously absurd, that without such a detailed account (hardly with it) no one could believe to have ever existed.

INDEX.

THE END.

ERRATA, &c.

Page vii. line 9, *for* is direct *read* is a direct
8,   26, *for* made *read* make
10,   20, *for* intenirìr *read* intenerìr
       26, *for* ĭntĕnĭrīr *read* ĭntĕnĕrīr
11,   29, *for* dwell *read* dwelt
21,   18, 19, *dele* parenthesis and all within it
36, last line, *for* unaccented *read* unacuted
42,   26, *dele* use
50,   15, *for* turned *read* slurred
51,   16, *for* new fangled *read* newly invented
       27, *for* quel *read* Quel
52,   13, *for* incensé *read* encensé
56,   8, *for* each *read* of which each
59,   16, *for* Πολλα μαλ' ὁσσ' *read* Πολλα μαλα ὁσσα
63,   4, *for* yet *read* you
64,   12, *for* est *read* et
65,   7, *for* est *read* et
       22, *for* n *read* u
66,   2, *for* prescribed *read* proscribed
75,   18, *for* difference *read* difficulties
89,   22, *for* dispartita *read* dipartita
91,   13, *for* ter *read* iter'
93,   7, *for* strangely *read* strongly
101,   21, *for* great *read* greater
102,   5, *for* words *read* words when
108,   3, *for* poet *read* poets
110,   12, *for* and *read* and of
       15, *for* on *read* in
112,   16, *for* of the three *read* of three
117,   4, *for* ολισσης *read* ολισση
121,   19, *for* dissyllabic *read* trisyllabic
123,   3, *for* καρτιστοις *read* καρτιστον
128,   14, *for* βιζριθι *read* βιβριθι
    last line, *for* may be *read* may well be
132,   16, *for* to *read* of
137,   7, *for* iambi *read* anapæsts
142,   10, *for* final *read* long final

ERRATA, &c.

Page 150, line 15, *for* observed *read* absurd

    154,   16, *for* verse *read* verses

    156,   7, *for* knows *read* knows that

    163,   19, *no break after* ā'dvĕntā'rĕ.

    164,   7, *for* four *read* three

                   9, *for* eight *read* seven

    166,   5, *for* any *read* have any

    167,   4, *for* seven lines of the first Georgic *read* nine lines of the fourth Eclogue

                   8, *for* seven *read* nine

                   9, *for* Georgic *read* fourth Eclogue

                12, *for* Lĭ'bĕr ĕt ā'lmă Cĕ'rĕs, &c. *read* Cā'stă fā'vĕ Lŭcĭ'nă, tū'ŭs jăm rē'gnăt Apōllo

    181,   15, *for* be *read* should be

    186, last line, *for* manner *read* manners

    192,   11, *for* ancient *read* in ancient

    195,   2, *for* person *read* person whom

                   4, *for* was *read* which was

    206,   13, *for* Sheke *read* Cheke

    213,   24, *for* αισχνισθι *read* αισχυνισθι

    237,   12, *for* περιστησασιν *read* περιστιχουσιν

For this long list of errata I must intreat the reader's pardon, and can only urge in extenuation, the incorrectness of copyists, and the multiplicity of marks above and below the lines. I perceive also, that in the hurry of arranging these papers for the press from different and voluminous manúscripts, written at various periods of time, some repetitions have crept in without my knowledge (compare p. 71. with p. 107. and p. 24. with p. 164.). For these and for any other oversights that may be found, I can the more confidently look to the reader's forgiveness, as a limited *circulation* for the purpose of criticism, and not *publication*, is the object for which these pages have been printed.

Any persons who may be disposed to favour the Author with their remarks, are requested to direct their letters under cover to Robert Price, Esq. M. P. Foxley, near Hereford.

For EU product safety concerns, contact us at Calle de José Abascal, 56–1°, 28003 Madrid, Spain or eugpsr@cambridge.org.

www.ingramcontent.com/pod-product-compliance
Ingram Content Group UK Ltd.
Pitfield, Milton Keynes, MK11 3LW, UK
UKHW010343140625
459647UK00010B/792